Explore Within

Explore Within

A JOURNEY TO INNER PEACE

N. T. Hettigei

ISBN-13: 978-1793137777
ISBN-10: 1793137773
Imprint: Independently published, 2019

True happiness is experiencing the bliss of being alive.
This is enabled by *responding* to every situation
rather than *reacting* to it.

\-   N. T. Hettigei

I dedicate this book to you

—

the explorer, philosopher, or sage.

Contents

Acknowledgments x

Preface xii

Chapter 1   Explorer 3

Chapter 2   Noble Heart 15

Chapter 3   Tree 29

Chapter 4   Sunset 39

Chapter 5   Satisfaction 49

Chapter 6   Happiness 59

Chapter 7   Philosopher 71

Chapter 8   Sage 83

Chapter 9   Inner Peace 95

Chapter 10 Vow 107

Recommended Readings 115

About the Author 117

Acknowledgments

I OWE PLENTY TO OTHERS who taught me many life lessons. This includes everyone I interact with either very closely—like my fatherly brother, caring wife, and admirable daughter—or at a far distance, like the teachers of ancient religions and current-day spiritual masters.

I would like to acknowledge you, the reader, who had no interaction with me in the past but did interact or will be interacting by reading this book. I sincerely believe that this will help you to live a blissful life. I acknowledge and thank you in advance for your openness, willingness, and effort in achieving your aspiration and determination to make this world a better place to live. Hence, I take this opportunity to recognize your noble effort of exploring inner peace.

Further, special thanks go to my friends who reviewed and edited my original manuscript and provided valuable comments that encouraged me to improve in my writing. A similar gratitude goes to my daughter, who encourages and inspires me to write and helped me tremendously to complete this book.

Preface

MOST OF US TEND TO be swayed by all that is happening around us. We rarely have the time to pause, pay attention, and reflect on our innermost responses to our own life. Most of us are unaware that every one of us is born with a noble heart to make us happy every second of our life.

This book offers a simple way to explore your approach to life and enables you to unlock the peace within. The practices outlined here benefits each one of us, regardless of the image you have chosen for yourself. In the course of this voyage of discovery, you will learn to recognize your true nature and how to enrich your life and live peacefully.

While the primary purpose of this book is to enhance the individual's experience of well-being, this is also an attempt to shape a peace-loving society to heal a world that is being divided by petty differences.

You will find a certain self-check to help you discover who you are and your pathway to inner peace. It will be helpful if you stop reading for a few minutes and try these exercises as you enjoy the breathtaking scenery on this wondrous journey.

I included certain restatements, similes, and pictorial representations throughout the book, hoping that they would resonate my message in you. Also, toward the end of this book, a list of recommended readings has been provided to further your understanding and advancement in this journey.

You may use this book as your lifestyle handbook and refer to it from time to time to experience your inner peace.

The unexamined life is not worth living.

—SOCRATES

CHAPTER 1

Explorer

WE HAVE BEEN EXPLORING EVERYTHING around us from the inception of mankind, individually and collectively. We explore the surrounding nature, cities, countries, continents, the globe, and now the universe, collectively. We share such knowledge among us, wishing goodness for mankind. Those explorations and discoveries are used for our benefit or detriment. Individually we explore things and activities around us and make our own world with a myriad of thoughts, perceptions, interpretations, and beliefs. With such perceptions we create our own self – self-image. We are slaves of our self-image created by our mind. We rarely examine inwardly and explore within to recognize our true nature.

As an explorer, you may have climbed mountains, traveled to many countries, and studied the globe and universe with much thrill and enthusiasm. This is because we are born with curiosity and our rudimentary quest for knowing more about things interesting to us. We extend our attention to external stimuli to make our world. However, exploring within and discovering our essence is hardly done, or even attempted. Here you are embarking on such a journey. The emotions, desires, and fears are the valleys and mountains in our self-landscape. This exploration is to discover them within and to understand the purpose of life.

As children, we repeatedly ask "Why?" following every answer we receive from our parents until they give up answering. We continue that quest even as adults, looking for answers externally without exploring our inner landscape. As adults, our questioning fades away only when we recognize the entire world is within us. When we realize that seeking satisfaction from outside is an endless exercise, we turn to exploring within. When we continue the journey of exploring within, we can experience inner peace. Then we see the world differently. We recognize that the world we knew was just our reactions to external stimuli. What I realized is, instead of reacting, we can respond to all stimuli, external or internal, and live a peaceful life. The purpose of our life is to recognize this reality to live blissfully.

Many people have examined their self-landscape with much enthusiasm and realized the true nature of life. They did it with great enthusiasm and an open mind. Only a few of them have shared that experience with others. You too can examine yourself with such enthusiasm and excitement to discover your inner peace and to share such experience with others. It will benefit you and the people around you too.

This journey is not a pursuit but an instant experience of inner peace – true happiness. Your pursuit of happiness will never end since your perception of happiness is changing. Perception and mind-based pursuit is a never-ending process. When you get there, your perception will change, and you will pursue more satisfaction or happiness. Does this sound familiar? Once you deeply realize this, you will turn to explore within. That makes you to pick this book to read.

Instead of exploring within, many people seek happiness from outside. In the pursuit of happiness, most of us look for satisfaction from accumulating material things and opinions of others. This is a fundamental mistake in your pursuit of happiness. If you believe satisfaction is happiness that is a never-ending exercise. Satisfaction depends on our perceptions. Since our perceptions change from one experience to another, we are never completely satisfied with any situation. The truth is individually we create our own world with many thoughts, memories, perceptions, interpretations, judgments, and beliefs. They are all accumulated from external sources. Hence, we live in misery and chaos with a self-image created by others' command and never be satisfied. In other words, we are still suffering from slavery, since we act upon others' opinions which speculated by our mind. We are in the chaos created by the enslaved mind which trying to make us someone who we are not - our self-image.

For example, consider your response to what you do for a living. You may either have a passion for your job or you may hate it. Your heart impels you to reflect on an issue, feel deeply about it, and eventually guide to act on it. However, while your heart offers such guides, it's your mind that pores over the implications of external events and reacts based on perception, belief, and fear. Many of us dwell on the mind rather than in the heart, which always guides us to be in peace. The mind blocks and obscures your heartfelt intention with myriad of thoughts, perceptions, beliefs, and fear of others' opinion on you. Since we distrust our intuition and the noble nature of our heart, we live in distress, agony, and fear. We unintentionally distract our need for well-being with our confusing thoughts and perceptions that are created by our enslaved mind. You may think you need to work and you have no choice. Your mind can not see any other option but to stick with your job while hating it. This is your enslaved mind talking and directing you through this situation.

In contrast, the more you begin to understand the way your heart responds to life's situations, the more you will be inclined to trust it. You may not have the choice or option to change your job. Yet you have the choice or option to respond to this situation differently, without being a slave of the mind. You can explore within to see what make you hate your job and correct the cause. You may not like your boss's attitude – friction – or you may think others are doing a better job by fixating to that idea – clinging. When you eliminate such friction and clinging you will be free from enslaved mind and you will start to love your job. You will learn a few techniques to manage your friction and clinging in the coming chapters. This will give you the confidence needed to draw on your inner peace and be happy. What I find immensely interesting is that the greater your understanding of the heart's nobility—its all-encompassing compassion and generosity—the better off you will be in all aspects. You will find yourself infinitely enriched in terms of your health, wealth, stability, and inner peace, which will influence your attitude toward the world at large. If you do not examine the depths of your heart, you cannot draw on inner peace. When you cannot draw on inner peace, you are bound to suffer from stress, problems, confusions, and disarrays.

While human beings have sought different ways of examining and understanding the heart's inherent nobility, many fall into mind-created traps. We need to identify those mind-created obstructions to our happiness. There are many methods used for this purpose from ancient times to this day. Such methods are taught in our spiritual doctrines, social ethics, and other peace-loving teachings.

Such variety is necessary to cater to people with different temperaments. That is why we see that different religions and teachings are accepted by a discrete group of people. However, I find that although the underlying temperament differs from person to person, the overarching approach to our life depends on the philosopher or sage in us. So, I see only two groups of people on this planet—some prominent with the philosophical approach and others with the insightful approach.

Those adopting the philosophical approach can be identified as philosophers, and the rest are sages. Whether you are one or the other depends on the degree of your receptivity to the heart's nobility and the extent to which you fathom its depths.

This book is merely an attempt to help you understand whether you are a philosopher or a sage and enable you to open your noble heart and unlock the peace within to enjoy true happiness. In other words, promote your well-being. This will allow you to reap the rewards of quality life that you so justly deserve, regardless of where you live or the circumstances of your life.

If you are a philosopher, you question most situations you encounter, searching for the best comprehensible answers to them based on your intellect. This approach ensures that the answer is equally compatible with the stirrings of your mind rather than your heart. If you are a sage, you first infer and experience the peace within and then relate to external conditions to reflect on their significance. I find many of us have qualities of both the philosopher and the sage in varying degrees.

According to the historians, the ancient Greeks always viewed a philosopher as an *eternal seeker of wisdom*: someone who always searches the truth, comes close to it, but ultimately cannot attain perfect wisdom. As opposed to a philosopher, the sage in ancient Greece was considered the *bearer of wisdom*— one who already possesses wisdom and only needs to self-actualize oneself. Whether you are a philosopher or a sage depends on the degree of your wisdom—which I would call *inner peace*. The wisdom or inner peace you bear is always with you no matter who you are. I find that irrespective of your approach as a sage or a philosopher, you can become a *bearer of wisdom* or, in other words, dwell in *inner peace*. Once you recognize the nobility of your heart, your wisdom flourishes. You will recognize the reality of things happening inside and outside with clarity and become a bearer of wisdom. At this stage, you may not see yourself as a philosopher or a sage; you could be one in-between them, with one prominent over the other.

Every human being has a longing for well-being. We take a different approach to seek this either as a philosopher or as a sage. You may not have labeled yourself as either of them, but as a human being, there is a philosopher and a sage in you. Most of us have both qualities; however, one is more prominent than the other. Depending on the style of approach and qualities in you, you become a philosopher or a sage. Understanding your approach to life helps you to draw on your inner peace to be happy. In other words, your well-being depends on the philosopher or sage within you. Once you recognize who you are, you can find your pathway to explore your inner peace. Those who have fathomed the potential that lies deep in their heart and explored the path that leads to the nobility of the heart have consequently achieved a peaceful and fulfilling life. Whether you are a philosopher or a sage, you could become a better one, depending on how thorough your understanding is of your heart's inherent nobility. As you become more intuitive about your heart's character, the peace that lies dormant within you will expand exponentially. This will help you, philosopher or sage, to understand how integral your noble heart is for your well-being.

Explore Within

I look to you as an explorer engaged in this effort to understand who you are and the noble nature of your heart – *inner peace.* Rest of the chapters in this book will assist you to penetrate either the philosopher or the sage in you. Through the insights thus gained, you will grasp the essential meaning of your life. Your curiosity to understand who you are will in turn serve as the driving force to find your inner peace. As you continue to read, please critically examine and undertake the various self-checks outlined throughout this book to get a firsthand experience of your heart. Your insight into the true nature of your noble heart will gradually grow and enable you to evolve into a better sage or philosopher. I welcome you to this expedition where you can recognize your true self to live blissfully.

To help you on your way, I have refrained from any mention of gender, race, or color that may unintentionally lead to an expression of bias or perception of discrimination. I have made it a point not to use limiting words like he, or she. Nor have I confined myself to a geographical location. My aim in deliberately avoiding these pitfalls is to build a bridge that will enable your noble heart to directly connect with the contents of this book, unhindered by prejudice. The basic intention here is to encourage you to keep an open mind to all possibilities, regardless of the characteristics that define the person you are—male or female, child or adult, rich or poor, black or white, able or challenged, and everything in between.

You need to set aside all such discriminatory identities

that you may have about yourself. Pay no attention to any of your self-identifications such as your nationality, race, creed, or even your gender. Be free from all such boundaries and open your mind to all possibilities. Imaging you are an infant who has no grasp of social and physical differences. This will open your noble heart. You will be released from the friction of all discriminatory perceptions. In this process, once you go beyond the identity of gender as well, you break through your enslaved mind. You are free and a sense of calmness will rush through your mind and body. I trust you can feel and recognize this phenomenon right now. Let go of all your identities and open heart to sense peace within you. Sense of lightness and free of agitation will surge through your inner peace. You touched your noble heart – *inner peace*. Relax on this condition and dwell in your noble heart as long as you can. This is your first level of experience of inner peace which is the bliss of being alive – true happiness.

While your own heart is unique to you, it is present in every living being on this earth. Your heart's nobility—*inner peace*—is within you, and you share that with all human beings and everything else on this earth and beyond. As you read, draw your inferences without prejudice, and absorb what is presented free of prior concepts. An open mind is fundamental to this expedition of self-discovery.

Explore Within

I welcome you the explorer, philosopher, or sage to this expedition, who is, above all, an important member of this evolving civilization who will carry forward a peaceful way of life. This discovery continues from generation to generation from ancient times. Many people discovered this by following a path defined by their religious teaching or the discipline of society, or certain individuals discovered this on their own. You could do the same.

As Socrates said, "The unexamined life is not worth living." We need to examine our life by exploring within. You had a glimpse of peaceful experience by letting go of perceptions – friction – of discriminatory identities. In the next few chapters, you will explore within to discover much more of who you are and your inner peace. I have no doubt that you are a great explorer, and in the not-too-distant future, you will share the experience of this discovery with many other philosophers and sages, including those who are yet to be born into this world.

*Inside each of us, there is a noble heart.
This heart is the source of our finest
aspiration for ourselves and the world.*

—VENERABLE 17TH KARMAPA

Explore Within

CHAPTER 2

Noble Heart

ALL HUMAN BEINGS ARE BORN with a noble heart, which is universal. Our mind obscures this universal truth and creates a self-image. We lose our inner peace to the myriads of thoughts and perception which we call the "mind." The mind is what emotionally reacts to an external situation, mulls over them, and distracts inner peace and identifies us as individuals. When we do not entertain thoughts leading to the perception of self-image, our inherited bliss will surge. That is the nobility of our heart buried deep within the reservoir of inner peace. We hardly experiencing it since we confine to our mind. We do not look beyond our mind rather many do not know that mind is another faculty. By distancing from our self-image – *the mind,* we can reveal the nobility of the heart and gradually travel deep into inner peace. You had a glimpse of the experience of your heart and inner peace by exercising the techniques we discussed in the last chapter. We will continue to explore within, probing so deeply without prejudice so we can recognize our self-image created by the enslaved mind for its worth, and thereby we will be able to distance from it to dwell in inner peace.

Aristotle was a Greek philosopher who is also considered one of the founders of Western philosophy. When he turned seventeen, he joined Plato's Academy in Greece and stayed until he was thirty-seven. His writings cover an incredible array of subjects including physics, metaphysics, poetry, theater, music, logic, rhetoric, politics, ethics, and even biology and zoology. One of his famous quotes about life is, "Educating the mind without educating the heart is no education at all." This brings us to our discussion about the firsthand experience that we need to have as an explorer. What Aristotle states here is that without experiential knowing—educating the heart—knowledge gathered through thinking and logical arguments are of no use. In other words, thoughts and perceptions that create our mind is just intellect, but our heartfelt experiences are intelligent. Therefore, I am prompting you to experience true happiness rather than providing information leading to your conceptual understanding of inner peace. You experienced inner peace when you withdraw your attention from all discriminatory identities including your gender. Experiencing means educating your heart. In my assessment, Aristotle too was a great philosopher who was a *bearer of wisdom* rather than common philosophers who are *seekers of wisdom*.

We bear wisdom in our heart. We are born with a noble heart full of joy and happiness. When we get older, this joy and.

happiness get evaded and replaced by our intellect that we gather from books and other's opinions. As adults we need to seek the joy and happiness that were apparent in us and enjoyed immensely in our childhood. This is because our thoughts, perceptions, and memories dominate us in our adulthood and obscure the noble nature of our heart which is always joyful and peaceful. We have an enslaved mind that obstructs our happiness, which is the noble nature of our heart

While on the subject, it is important to clarify that the heart and mind to which I am referring throughout are not the organs—*heart and brain*—within our bodies that keep us functioning physically. On the contrary, the heart is the alertness, or our essence as human beings, and the mind is the thoughts, perceptions, and memories that react to life situations. Our essence is always calm and peaceful and responds to situations without reacting to them emotionally. Our mind is full of thoughts that perceive the world based on memories and past experiences. Our heart is full of emotions, mostly manipulated by our enslaved mind. However, our *noble heart* is free from all types of emotion but is full of bliss. Once bliss springs from our inner peace, our heart becomes a noble heart. True happiness is that inner peace surging through our heart as bliss, which is noble. So, I call it *Noble Heart*.

As humans, we are to be aware of many things in us and in our

surroundings. Modern humans are known as "*homo sapiens, sapiens*" because we know we have a thinking mind. That means we are capable of identifying our *mind* from our heart. When we say "heartfelt," what we mean is our attention recognizes the incident without any preconceived thoughts or perceptions or any help from the mind. Most of the time, we act on our mind's direction rather than on our heart's direction or consciousness. If we are aware—*use our attention wisely*—we use our noble heart, which is free of all kinds of emotions but is full of bliss. Our awareness, consciousness, or heart is a synonym for our wise attention.

Our enslaved mind is what makes us agitated with emotion. This enslaved mind is what labels us as an individual, which brings us sorrow or short-lived pleasure or satisfaction. We can be aware or conscious of these desolations. But we may not know how to deal with them. We may temporarily suppress them, but they will resurface without any warning. In contrast, our heart loves peace and bliss, but our mind does not allow us to sustain that blissfulness. If this idea puzzles you, be patient; we will explore this further through this wondrous expedition with wise attention to inner peace.

Have you ever wondered why our eyes get wet when we feel joy or sorrow? On one occasion, I found myself observing the difficulties faced by a physically challenged person trying to get into a wheelchair. My help was accepted with gratitude, as evidenced by the person's expression—tears in eyes—and appreciation with words of thank-you! The impact of the incident on me was quite amazing. Unremarkable though the incident was, it brought bliss to my heart, joy to my mind, and tears to eyes of both of us. What an incredibly powerful impression that little episode made on both that person and me! The nobility that had lain dormant in our hearts generated such bliss within; its impact caused our eyes to well up with tears.

This could, however, be interpreted as an unremarkable incident. Instead, reconsider the situation; a person who needed help appreciated my help and expressed gratitude after the help was rendered. The instinctive responses—tears—is not a biological process triggered by preconceived perceptions. It is an expression of the noble nature of the heart. We did not push that with thoughts or past experience, it surges within us effortlessly. Stay with this notion as long as you can. You will touch your inner peace.

However, one can interpret this as a bodily reaction through certain hormonal changes that surfaced through eyes in the form of tears. That is your gathered knowledge or intellectual interpretation. A common philosopher may concur with such interpretation

A sage may offer an entirely different interpretation of the same incident. A sage interprets the tears as a stream of bliss evoked in both persons' inner essence—the *noble heart*. A sage would see the tears as an expression of the nobility inherent in the hearts of both people without any preconceived concept. The true, noble nature of the heart endorses a connection between the two people. It leads them to exchange their innermost uniqueness, which proves without a doubt that the heart is, indeed, noble and common to both parties. The tears are merely a physical manifestation of the joy and happiness—*bliss*—an expression of inner peace. The noble nature of the heart—*wise attention*—is like crystal-clear water in a lake where you can see the bottom of it with no obstructions. Also, with the nobility of the heart—*when you have wise attention*—you can respond to situations without emotional impact just like hills, trees, and a cloudy sky can reflect on the still water without making any ripples.

The purpose here is simply to provide you with an appropriate example that will ensure a more in-depth understanding of what I mean by a *noble heart.* Some call the expression of the heart as gut feelings, referencing intuition that comes from our innermost essence. I use the term *wise attention* as our innermost essence—*noble heart.* Our heart can be on a variety of different realms. When we have wise attention—the *nobility of our heart*—we are directly connected with inner peace. If we are attentive to our inner peace, we recognize our *noble heart,* which is full of bliss. Surrounding thoughts, perceptions, and emotions disturb our bliss. We can see all that is happening around us are mere vibrations or fleeting changes. When our attention is invested in the vibrations created by our thoughts and perceptions, we suffer. When we redirect our attention back to inner peace wisely, we move away from such suffering. With wise attention we can dwell in inner peace and live blissfully.

Try recalling a similar incident in your life that moved

you to tears. It does not have to be a happy one. You may, for instance, have wept when you lost someone close to you. I urge you to focus on that moment of bereavement and try recalling the instinctive feelings you experienced at that time. It may be dormant, but it is still within you and will rise to the surface if you allow it. That heartfelt moment boiling inside may impact you as same or much stronger than you had it on the day you first felt it, and the result would be tears, or at least a feeling of sorrow. If, however, you did fail to connect with your heart's nobility at that significant moment, that memory would have been lost. If so, try to dwell on a joyful moment that you can recall and experience the same result again and again. They are not your gathered knowledge; they are the experiences that reside in your heart. It is intelligent, not intellect.

In brief, we all are aware of the soft corner within us, which is our inherited compassion as human beings. We often ignore this since we enslave our mind and lack wise attention. The soft corner in us surfaces from time to time, regardless of the kind of situation—joyful or sorrowful—in which we find our deeper essence. At the surface level, we can see this when a mass-scale disaster occurs in any corner of the world. The devastation is shared with compassion by all of us. Many weep together and go to the extent of volunteering their time and resources with compassion. At a deeper level, we need to recognize this as the universally unique nature of the noble heart or inner peace in every human being. I hope you can see what I am referencing to as *wise attention* as the *noble heart* and again *noble heart* to *inner peace*. I am drawing this equation because when it comes to our inner peace, it can be identified only with attention clear of any thoughts of perceptions—*wise attention*. When you are free from thoughts and perceptions, there is no interpretation to differentiate our attention from awareness, consciousness, or inner peace. All of them are equal, and some call this a universal energy field, but I prefer to call it inner peace which is our wise attention.

Also, try to dwell on a joyful moment that you can recall. You will have the same results. This time you may be able to clearly notice the difference between your thinking mind and the noble heart. You were joyful with no interruptions from any thoughts or perceptions. You were fully attentive to that joy and happiness; hence there is no influence from the mind. With this you may recognize the bliss in you. The longer you can keep your attention, the more bliss will prevail in you, and your eyes may well up with tears. I trust you can experience this blissful moment right now. Once your attention has moved out from this blissful inner peace, the enslaved mind will take over your attention and direct it to a painful past and fearful future. Therefore, we should ensure our attention is wisely directed— *use the noble nature of our hearts.*

Whether a king or a commoner, the richest or the poorest, the inner peace is something we share universally. At the same time, it is unique to each one of us when seen through our minds. Therefore, it is difficult to recognize, or it can only be seen with some limitations. To our mind, inner peace is the nobility of our heart. We need wise attention to recognize our *inner peace* when it surfaces within us in the form of bliss.

We are exploring this noble heart's universal nature—*nobility* or *inner peace*—on this inner exploration as it exists within us and is fundamental to all living beings. You can see similar reference in the venerable seventeenth Karmapa's book *The Heart Is Noble: Changing the World from the Inside Out*. In the first paragraph of its first chapter "Our Shared Ground," he states:

> *Inside each of us, there is a noble heart. This heart is the source of our finest aspiration for ourselves and the world. It fills us with the courage to act on our aspirations. Our nobility may be obscured at times, covered over with small thoughts or blocked by confused and confusing emotions. But a noble heart lies intact within each of us nonetheless, ready to open and be offered to the world... When we clear away all that blocks it, this heart can change the world.*

The above-mentioned book was a result of the author's interaction with a group of young, intelligent, American university students. It was written as answers to the new generation and endorses the fact that we share our noble heart without any geographical, social, or ethnic boundaries.

Philosophers find their inner peace—*nobility of the heart*—after searching and mulling over many subjects before finally seeing it deep within.

To gain an in-depth understanding of this truth, as you continue to read, keep an open mind and recognize the response emanating from a deeper level within you. Do not allow your preconceived concepts and doubt to obscure the message. We need inner peace, just as we need oxygen in the air that we share with each other to survive in this world. This sense of sharing the peace you feel right now is your very own, and it is coming from the deepest level common to all of us. Do not doubt and suppress it with your thoughts and perceptions. Let that sense of bliss to come through inner essences. You will experience true happiness.

The philosopher Rene Descartes's (1596–1650) best-known statement "*I think; therefore, I am*" may have come about after recognizing the noble heart that is common to us all and the realization that we create a self-image with thoughts. In fact, that statement is known as *the Cogito* which in Latin is "*dubito, ergo cogito, ergo sum,*" that is, "*I doubt; therefore, I think. Therefore I am.*" We doubt our noble heart and act on our mind's directions, which creates our self-image. Many of us fear to act on our gut feelings or intuition coming from our deeper sense, merely because we doubt the power of our noble heart.

Therefore, keep an open mind, without conceptualized doubts, and be wisely attentive to intuition sparks within you. That is very important to any circumstance in our life, as it is for our well-being. When we encounter compassion and empathy, equanimity stems from our inner essence; we should not doubt it and let it slip away from our attention. We must be vigilant for all signs and signals coming from our noble heart to make our life blissful and happy. Our enslaved mind brings thoughts, perceptions, doubt, and fear of those signs and creates our ever-changing self as individuals, disguising the deepest level of our universal nature—*inner peace.*

Whatever you learned through your heartfelt experiences is truly intelligent. If you conceptualize based on your thought process, it is a subjective intellect that can change with your fleeting thoughts and perceptions. My assessment is that Aristotle comprehended this fact with his inner experience and stated, "Educating the mind without educating the heart is no education at all." Consequently, I will try to educate your heart in the next two chapters. You will find some discussion and exercises on how to recognize your true nature and experience the nobility of your heart by being with nature.

*Look deep into nature, and then you will
understand everything better.*

—ALBERT EINSTEIN

CHAPTER 3

Tree

WHEN WE WERE BORN, we were alert and totally attentive. You may
have seen some babies born with their eyes wide open and alert
to see what is happening around them. You see joy and happiness in their eyes. Those babies cry only when hungry. The
other type of babies cry as soon as they see the light of this
planet, mainly because they too were alert yet scared and terri-
fied to see the new world. We are born with alertness – *wise attention.* I always wondered whether there is a connection between the type of these newborns to approach to our lives—as a
philosopher or a sage.

You may have noticed that when a plant is growing, it is alert
to the light and warmth of the sun. They grow toward the sun-
light. Some plants and trees are very alert throughout the day,
tilt toward the sun during the day; they wake-up at dawn and go
to sleep in the dusk. The entire world around us is alert and
awake in every moment and enjoying the liveliness and blissfulness in the surroundings. Except perhaps many of us humans,

who are slaves of our minds. Many of us do not find this bliss-fulness and liveliness in nature. We need to be attentive and look deeper to see the liveliness in a tree standing in front of us.

Albert Einstein, who lived from 1879 to 1955 AD, is known around the world for his scientific discoveries and the hardship he endured during his life. Einstein shared a lot of wisdom and insight on life, people, and the world in general. His conclusion was that you will understand everything around and within you better when you look deep into nature, and he stated, "Look deep into nature, and then you will understand everything better." This is his famous quote even though he was a philosopher of science. On a special note, Einstein's philosophical thinking was driven by the solution of problems first encountered in his work in experimental physics. He is known as a great physicist as well with his hallmark theory of special relativity equation of $E=mc^2$.

I came across the simplest explanation for Einstein's equation given by Sadhguru—born in 1948—one of the great sages in the present days. It became clear to me that Einstein was a scientist who bears the wisdom, when Sadhguru reveals the following in his book *Inner Engineering: A Yogi's Guide to Joy*:

When Einstein gives us the formula $E=mc^2$, he is, put it simply, saying that everything in the universe can be seen as just one energy. Religions all over the world have been proclaiming the same thing using somewhat different terminology when they assert that "God is everywhere.".

So, Einstein's statement of "Look deep into nature, and then you will understand everything better" should not be taken lightly. It has a profound meaning that was a result of his own experience in his work of physics. We can examine this further by exploring physics in nature.

As children we all learned a lot from nature. You may recall watching butterflies flying around and landing on beautiful flowers at will with no selective order. You may have curiously observed a procession of ants marching on the path they themselves created. Nature was once our teacher; we experienced many miracles of nature, being there and marveling with no concern of time. In this age of information, as a child, you may not have had a chance to observe and enjoy such beauty and learn from this kind of experience. Either way, we can discuss and elevate such learning on this exploration of inner peace. We can start by looking at a tree as a part of nature. You may easily ignore its connectedness to our existence.

Contemplate on a tree as a living being. It stands tall like a giant, and its mighty structure is visible to all who gaze on it. With the arrival of autumn, it sheds its leaves and stays in a dormant state all through winter. With the advent of spring, leaves and buds sprout on its branches, and summer sees them blossom. The tree grows leaves and flowers and bears fruit until the following autumn, just like a human being waking up in the morning with the purpose of being active during the day and retiring

31

for the night to rest before the next day dawns. Compare a tree with a human by equating a year in human life as a day in a plant's life. In other words, the three hundred days that represent a tree's life span would translate into three hundred years in human life. Would your instincts tell you to consider this reality? Do you find the idea fascinating? This fascination should bring a sense of calmness to you. Dwell on your calmness to experience the inner peace that you share with a tree.

You may, flatly deny this, and perhaps you don't see a tree as anything other than a mere commodity, available for humans to utilize for their comfort. A tree, you may contend, provides shade and fruit during the summer and firewood in winter. The branches, strong and solid, merely represent another product that can be utilized to satisfy many needs. Humans have, in fact, used the tree, a readily available natural resource, in the past and will continue to do so in the future. Therefore, you do have reasons to deny that it is a living being and has any connection to your inner peace.

Leave your deepest instinct open to both possibilities—of the tree as a living being and as a commodity. Listen to the message it conveys to you. What does it say? Pay close attention to what your mind and heart have to say about these ideas. You may simply accept the notion of a tree as a living being or find yourself challenging its validity with a series of questions. Whatever response you finally settle on will offer an interesting insight into the depths of your heart and, consequently, your approach to life as a philosopher or a sage. Distinguish the true nature of your heart that has often been misinterpreted as the workings of your mind. It constitutes a fascinating experience. I wonder if you have recognized the philosopher in you challenging the validity of the tree as a living being. If not, and you see the life of a tree is similar to yours, qualities of a sage are prominent in you.

Of the many questions that are likely to arise in your mind, the initial ones would probably include, "What kind of an idea is this? How can I and nature be interconnected?" You may be seeking answers to those questions, just as philosophers do for every quest that comes to mind. Your desire to seek answers is an expression of the philosopher in you. Read on, and you will certainly find the answers to the questions I have suggested, along with answers to other questions that will arise as you explore within, as outlined in each page of this book. Those very answers will help you recognize inner peace, as well as the many other answers you may need for many questions in your life.

Reconsider a tree as a living being like you. It stands still, yet alive and vibrant, calm and sturdy, not bothered by wind or surrounding conditions. Can you be like that—not reacting to external stimuli that are extrapolated with the stream of thoughts and perceptions that bring misery to your life? Nevertheless, can you relate to the liveliness and calmness of a giant tree? Here is an exercise in recognizing nature's freshness and calmness:

While walking in the wood or park, still your mind and embrace the surrounding freshness by spreading your attention beyond your conventional boundaries. Spread your attention to trees in front and back of you. You do not have to look around, just spread your attention to all trees and space in between them. You should sense at your deepest level, the joy and happiness that trees and shrubs relish by being still and sturdy. With your breath, you may bring in that calmness and aliveness in nature into your body. You may feel the joy and happiness filling in your mind and body that you share with surrounding trees. Try this for a few times to see whether you can embrace the liveliness in nature. Make this a habit whenever you are out walking in the wood or park.

You may find the joy and happiness that stems from this exercise are quite different from your preconceived perception of what is joy or happiness. This is the *bliss* that you share with the trees, shrubs, and any other living being in this world. Do not mistake it for *satisfaction,* which formulates around the mind-created perceptions.

Everything in nature is filled with bliss, which is the same energy that we experience. When you cut a branch of a tree, the same energy heals the scar from it like a cut in your skin heals without any treatment. If you set aside all scientific explanations of how a wound gets healed without treatment, you will be able to recognize that the tree also shares the same energy as you do. Some call this an energy field in the liveliness, which is common to everything and every being on this planet. This energy makes such miracles like healing wounds and sicknesses. I find that they are referring to the bliss in us as the energy field in liveliness.

The bliss emerging from inner peace heals us and all living beings on this planet and beyond. We need to recognize this fact and allow such healing to occur without any interruption from our enslaved mind. This bliss is the universal energy field summarized in Einstein's equation of $E=mc^2$, which I like to call the inner peace.

We need to develop the habit of paying attention to this energy field—*inner peace*—that allow us to be happy without getting depressed, becoming insane, and being a slave of our mind. Freshness and liveliness in nature are inner peace emerging everywhere and in you. If you pay attention to liveliness in nature, it will lead you to inner peace just as the day gradually gets brighter with the sunrise.

> Pause for a moment and contemplate your inner response on the idea that we are all connected to nature and live and die eventually. Nature is changing as we change every second, minute, hour, day, week, month, and year. Every plant, creature, and thing, even rocks and mountains in nature sprout from space, grow, and die just like us human beings. We all are in the same pickle, carrying the same sour taste of suffering and fragile life.

When you look at this big picture relatively, you are just a minute creature in this world. If you are an ant, a bucket of water is a tsunami. When you are a child, your dad is a giant. If you are an elephant, rain is just a shower you take every day. Is this idea petrifying or fascinating? This is a deeper measurement that reveals the degree to which your heart is open. If you are fascinated with this relative comparison, you live with wisdom rather than seeking wisdom through knowledge. Spend a few minutes sensing your wisdom; your inner peace in you is like flowers and plants smiling at you with morning dew. Dwell in the sensation surged in you and enjoy the beauty in your inner landscape. Get in touch with true happiness.

If we are attentive, we will see the liveliness in nature, and in our deepest sense of inner peace. We too love the freshness and calmness surging from nature. When we are calm and peaceful, our life will fill with bliss and happiness, the nobility of our heart. All we need is to find a way to redirect our attention from our enslaved mind to the bliss in us to dwell in inner peace. You could do this right now. Look at a plant or a tree in your vicinity and embrace the calmness emanating from it. If not, gaze at the leaves and branches on the front cover picture of this book and embrace a similar calmness and peacefulness surging in you.

We will work on Einstein's wisdom of nature along with a natural phenomenon that forces us to pause and dwell in inner peace in the next chapter.

*The present moment is filled with joy
and happiness.
If you are attentive, you will see it.*

—VENERABLE THICH NHAT HANH

Explore Within

CHAPTER 4

Sunset

A SUNSET IS A BREATHTAKING sight, isn't it? It is an amazing natural phenomenon, and almost anybody in the world will stop to enjoy such wondrous sight. When I say *stop*, I mean physically and mentally. I mean that at such moments, we need to pause our constantly flowing stream of thoughts and exclude extraneous musings, for a few moments, to focus on what has attracted our attention. Our attention will instantly draw to that wondrous sight and free us from all mind-created miseries.

Consider what is likely to happen when you contemplate on a colorful and wonderful sunset. It may stir memories of a sunset you admired in the past, but you may not recall its splendid colors clearly. Focus, instead, on the joyful moment you savored as you paused in your steam of thoughts to concentrate on the wondrous sight. What is crucially important here is that pause. The magnificence of the spectacle would probably have made you pause longer than you did at the sight of a tree or a plant that you came across earlier. A significant period of time would have elapsed between your first sight of the sunset—subject—and the moment you began thinking about it in analytical terms. That is the space of calmness or happiness.

This is where your true happiness lies, the space that you recognized in between the pause and the beginning of your thoughts about the sunset. This space between every activity gives us a moment of thoughts free period of happiness. When we are free from thoughts, we distance ourselves from our enslaved mind that brings us unhappiness. Once we break our silence by moving our attention from that space and stillness within us—inner peace—the happiness we enjoyed fades away. With a myriad of thoughts sprouting in our mind we distract our happiness and shift our attention from being blissful and happy to seek satisfaction.

Interrupt your reading for a second to ponder your heart's response to a colorful sunset. Focus your full attention on the sky. What an amazing display of nature's beauty it was; in fact, it's so glorious that it can rob you, for one precious instant, of speech and wipe all extraneous thoughts from your mind! By banishing the clamor of such reflections from your mind, momentarily, it allows inner peace to manifest as an expression of the blissful moment. Embracing the beauty and color of the sunset, you may yearn to be a part of that moment and, thereby, be one with nature. You may turn to the cover page of this book and focus on the colorful sky to practice this exercise.

However, at this point, a stray thought like "Do I feel this way all the time?" is likely to cut short your retreat. The next series of questions you ask yourself may be "Where am I? Where was I going? Why did I stop?" In other words, your mind could just urge you to go back to reading or to whatever activity you were engaged in before that blissful moment.

The important point is that for a moment, you did interrupt the stream of thoughts that dominate you and dive deep into the core of your heart, which is forever still, silent, and peaceful. That pervasive stillness prompted you to pause and kept your restlessness in check. The emerging bliss held the usual stream of thoughts at bay.

However, after that pause, brief or lengthy, you reconnected with your age-old habit of creating the stream of thoughts passing through your mind. The philosopher in you may have contemplated the beauty of the spectacle and wondered over its splendor; you may have expressed your amazement at the variety of colors a sky can display at sunset. You would have thought this everyday phenomenon a rare event. You may enjoy the beauty of the sky's hues—red, orange, or peach, set off by a streak of brilliant, fiery yellow—and yet remain at a distance, observing the sunset as nothing but a natural phenomenon that is alien to your immediate life. While regarding it as something quite remote, taking place far away, and of little direct relevance to you, you may still find the setting sun interesting enough to make you pause for at least a fraction of a second. That is your noble heart's effort to surge through your thoughts. You need to develop a habit to recognize such events.

This sight may trigger memories of your science lessons about the composition of the sun's rays. The more you analyze a subject, the greater the distance it creates between you and that special moment you experienced so deeply – *inner peace*. In this state of mind, questions and answers may rush to take over, forcing the blissful experience that made you pause for a moment to fade away. Your inquiring mind predominates. The inevitable result is that content with what you have seen, you are likely to move on with your life and disregard the insight you gained into the power of your noble heart. Considering life to be more satisfying and stimulating than the moment during which you halted your stream of thoughts, your mind may take you away from that deeply felt moment of bliss.

Once again, I urge you to return to that moment. Observe the feeling of tranquility evoked simply by contemplating on the sunset. Yes, do pause for a few seconds; allow the feeling of bliss to rise within you. Embrace the silence and stillness that lie around and within you—*inner peace*. During this brief span of time, you will feel yourself to be a part of nature and continue to enjoy the beauty of the moment that now appears more stimulating than anything else around you including fleeting satisfaction. As you pause to contemplate its beauty, prevent other thoughts from crowding into your mind, and you will observe the duration of that blissful pause gradually increasing. As a result, you will find yourself embracing the moment more closely and dwelling in inner peace. This is the bliss that rises from the depths of your noble heart – true happiness.

Cherishing the moment in this manner, you will feel yourself as an integral part of this natural phenomenon and stay with it longer. The bliss that fills your mind leaves no room for distracting thoughts to your happiness. So powerful is its pull, you may forget what you were doing and where you were going. Since this bliss dominates both your heart and your mind, the two become inseparable. You will experience the nobility of your heart and cherish with joy and happiness. Try it now and see whether the experience is as absorbing for you as I trust it will be.

Plato was another Greek philosopher who famous for his works together with his mentor, Socrates, and his student, Aristotle, during the period of 428–347 BC. Plato is known as the most influential philosopher of all time. He perhaps provided the main opposition to the Materialist view of the world. When he said that "You can discover more about a person in an hour of play than in a year of conversation," he implied that discovery is to be experiential than conceptual. Plato is a great philosopher in everyone's eyes. The greatness comes with the open mind and nobility of the heart that he had demonstrated in many of his works. In my view, Plato's statement tells us that he promoted experiential knowledge rather than logical arguments. That is why he stated that "an hour of play" is greater than "years of conversation" with a person to discover more about that person. So, even if the philosopher in you dominates your mind, you need to be free from it and have an open mind to experience the reality and to learn more about a person, nature, and yourself.

I recently watched a documentary on Jun Kaneko, a famous Japanese ceramic artist who came to the United States in 1963 at the age of twenty-one. He said that he did not speak English. He learned English, studied, and graduated from Chouinard Art Institute in Los Angeles, California. His work is now included in more than forty museum collections around the world. In this documentary, he mentioned that the key to his success was keeping an open mind. In his words he is a free thinker, not scared of what others might think or say, and that gives him the gift of fearless creativity. He teaches his students by asking them to observe attentively what he is doing rather than enforcing any concept or principle of art on them.

He wants his students to be like him and create fearlessly without any preconceived system or method. When he refers to "open mind," what came to my attention was a mind without conceptual thinking, not an enslaved mind—in other words an open heart. He distances his enslaved mind and lets the intuition from inner peace blossom into innovations and creations. He dwells on the noble nature of his heart—*inner peace*—to innovate and create. In other words, he creates when he is in the zone, that is, inner peace. So keep all mud and debris—

44

thoughts and perceptions—off the lake—*mind*—so the pure and clear water—*bliss*—can spring from the bottom of your heart. You will be in "the zone," which is a long pause from the myriad of thoughts and confusions.

Most of us follow the directions from the enslaved mind, and as a result, we doubt and continue to live with stress, problems, confusion, and disarray. We can distance our enslaved mind by recognizing the bliss within us, which surfaces from time to time like it happened when you pause to enjoy the wondrous sunset. In fact, you did touch a glimpse of it with exercises you tried earlier. When you allow that bliss to grow in you, you can examine the depths of your heart and enter the zone or dwell in inner peace. Great sports players respond during a play, in a split second, without thinking, by following their intuition. When they are in the zone they respond to intuition with no interruption from thoughts, perception, and fear. So, they distance their enslaved mind when they are in the zone. You could do the same to win the challenges in your life.

Human beings have sought different ways to be in the zone or to distance their enslaved mind and recognize their heart's inherent nobility—*inner peace*. Among them, there are two primary approaches that I mentioned earlier: logical thinking or the approach of a philosopher, and experiential approach of a sage. When you explore with either of these approaches, you can open your heart to reveal inner peace. It will allow you to reap the rewards of your life that you so justly deserve, regardless of the unique circumstances of your life.

If a philosopher's approach is prominent in you, you

question most situations you encounter, searching for the best logical answers based on your perceptions. This approach sees that the answer is equally compatible with the stirrings of your mind rather than your heart. If you are using the approach of a sage, you first infer on the peace within and then relate it to the external conditions. I trust you have an inclination of who you are now and feel your heart's nobility—*inner peace*. This is irrespective of whether you see yourself as a philosopher or a sage. The inner peace surges through you as bliss or true happiness. However, when your enslaved mind seeks satisfaction, inner peace is obscured with a myriad of confusing thoughts and perceptions.

As Thich Nhat Hanh aptly said in his book *Peace Is Every Step: The Path of Mindfulness in Everyday Life*, "The present moment is filled with joy and happiness. If you are attentive, you will see it." That is the present moment which is filled with unconceptualized joy and happiness—*inner peace*. Our mind obscures this and takes us on a ride of misery or fleeting satisfaction—*conceptualized happiness*.

Fundamentally, what this means is you now know to what extent you seek happiness or satisfaction. If bliss is prominent in you, you dwell in your noble heart and happiness is inevitable. When seeking satisfaction, you are a slave of your mind. To be certain, we may need to analyze and explore this further. In the following chapters, we will be exploring the satisfaction and happiness for it worth to recognize its relevance to our well-being.

The secret of happiness, you see, is not found in seeking more, but in developing the capacity to enjoy less.

—SOCRATES

CHAPTER 5

Satisfaction

FOR MOST PEOPLE, HAPPINESS is a fleeting satisfaction. What we need to recognize is that happiness should be lasting pleasantness rather than a short-lived satisfaction based on our fleeting perceptions. Our perceptions are the result of our memories we entertained with our thoughts. When you think, "I am old" or "I am young," you become old or young as you perceived in your mind. Likewise, we seek satisfaction based on our perceptions. Recalling previous experiences or memories that gave birth to the original perception, we instantly seek more satisfaction. Therefore, satisfaction is relative to our perceived state of mind. But true happiness is blissful and free of fleeting perceptions.

When you think, it is your mind that engages in the process. Therefore, your needs and wants are created within your mind, according to your perceptions. These perceptions are the result of the analysis or questions you entertained earlier, and they direct your mind to seek satisfaction based on memories.

Depending on your perception of needs or wants, the level of satisfaction you gain may vary. But they are not really yours. They are built upon perceptions you accumulated from others opinions and external stimuli. None of them are what your heart wants or needs. Your heart needs peacefulness and wants to be happy. Therefore, you should distance from mind made chaos which includes your pursuit of satisfaction.

I hope you have already noticed that thinking or seeking satisfaction will not bring lasting happiness. If you allow yourself to probe deeper, you will conclude that the satisfaction does not give you the peace of mind or happiness that you sought in the first place. Once you are satisfied with one thing, you seek another, looking for greater satisfaction. You can never be happy in your pursuit of fleeting satisfaction. It's a trick of your enslaved mind to keep you away from your inner peace – *true happiness*.

Pause for a moment and reflect on the satisfaction you have sought so far in your life: Is it as fulfilling as you had imagined it to be? You may think you have everything that you want. Still are you truly happy with your life? In your desire to save the planet, you may assume that the target of your quest is, indeed, noble. But if you think deeply enough, in retrospect, you will realize that what you really wanted was to shape your self-image. Having made a change in what you perceived as wrong, you would be proudly proclaiming, "I did this," or "I created that." But your rudimentary motive would have been to satisfy yourself by claiming victory. Is that satisfaction truly noble and brings lasting happiness? The act of fulfilling your needs, the kind you consider helpful to your life or to that of others, generates a self-centered satisfaction. In some cases, such satisfaction may be low or even nonexistent, when perceived by others.

This means that when you define satisfaction, it is in relation to your self-image. Satisfaction is what the mind pursues at every moment but often fails to achieve. Driven by its lack of success in attaining the highest levels of satisfaction, the mind persists in its quest. This situation is comparable to that of philosophers who seek answers to every question that arises in their minds and, thwarted in their efforts, end up asking still more questions in their perennial quest for satisfaction. This pursuit brings stress and unhappiness. The miseries created through this process never ends. Since we are seeking happiness through fleeting satisfaction, we end up with getting quite the opposite—unhappiness.

The quest for satisfaction is perennial...

We cling to the conceptual desire or craving for social status, comfort, lust, and even peace and seek satisfaction. These are our longings born through clinging to thoughts and perceptions on external and internal searing throughout our life. Your search for higher social status by clinging to the perception of what others may think of you is an external searing. Your looking for comfort by changing your pillow with the perception that it will satisfy you is internal searing. That comfort will last only a few minutes and will lead you to seek more comfort, and in the end, it will make you unhappy.

The famous British philosopher John Stuart Mill, who lived in the nineteenth century, who was a proponent of utilitarianism, adopted the wisdom of the ancient Greeks. When it comes to happiness, instead of inundating his life with desire, Mill believed in simplicity. He believed in using things for a purpose, and if they served no purpose, if they were not needed, he banished them from his life. His famous saying "I have learned to seek my happiness by limiting my desires, rather than in attempting to satisfy them" comes from self-actualization. We try to be happy by satisfying our desires whether they are mundane or noble. Within an enslaved mind happiness is always far away, satisfaction is much closer, and we pursue it by clinging to our fleeting thoughts and perceptions.

We often accumulate many things and perceptions, seeking satisfaction. Those satisfactions fade away when we realize that seeking satisfaction is an endless exercise. We will settle in or cease seeking when we realize satisfying desires do not make us happy. Neither any material fulfillment nor achievements of any kind bring us lasting happiness. You may have heard about many unsatisfied scholars, millionaires, addicts, or activists who are now seeking happiness elsewhere, such as in ancient teachings or in spiritual practices.

It is true that the mind is the creator of many things in this world. The human mind is meant to support our intuition, and in doing so, it creates many things to help us. Often, the result falls short of the goal since perceptions get in the way. As you already know, the mind does not cease its effort; it keeps creating things, some of which are helpful, and others which are harmful to lives on this planet. In brief, satisfaction is subject to perception and therefore short lived since it is formulated within our mind. Satisfaction lasts until your next perception. Our perceptions change rapidly, since the base for them is fleeting thoughts.

Many philosophers will continue to think and question until they realize that conceptual wisdom is not worthy. Then they turn inward to see answers. It is possible for this to become a reality, because great philosophers are prepared to recognize opposites, willing to keep an open mind. With their inward approach, they refuse to be constrained by fleeting perceptions or the desire for mere satisfaction. However, many of us—*amateur philosophers*—are driven by the desire to be different from others—*ego*. This is because we cling to thoughts and perceptions which uplift our self-image. Great philosophers are open minded and free of prejudice and try not to cling to any specific ideal. In other words, their focus is on observing the self-image instead of seeking satisfaction, like enjoying the surrounding scenery of the valley – self-landscape - from higher ground to become a bearer of wisdom.

We need to cultivate the habit of observing the self-image more often and identify bliss in us and follow it to dwell in inner peace. It is like, instead of climbing every mountain, we should marvel at the surrounding beauty from the sky of the valley of our self-landscape. Until we evolve to that level by uplifting our attention—*wise attention*—the self-image will continue to form within the enslaved mind, and we will be in the never-ending pursuit of satisfaction.

What distinguishes you from a great philosopher is your ignorance of the difference between the heart and the mind. You believe that your mind has a satisfying answer to every question. The truth, however, is that your mind is only temporarily satisfied for a given period of time because it cannot think beyond your memories and perceptions. Sooner or later, it will begin to ask more questions and seek satisfaction again on a subject to which you believed you had all the answers. This will continue until you realize that satisfaction is not the happiness that you pursue.

So, while you may stop again to admire a colorful sunset

and pause for a moment to reflect on a tree, focus on the bliss springing in you. Experience the peacefulness and calmness in you. It could bring you to the realization that thinking or seeking satisfaction is not the ultimate purpose of life. If you allow yourself to probe deeper, you will conclude that the satisfaction does not give you the peace of mind that you seek.

It's not as if a sage is immune to being carried away by the momentary satisfaction derived from a particular sight or object. However, in such cases, the duration of the sage's enjoyment or the time lost in seeking further satisfaction will be considerably drawn out. Sooner or later, the sage's noble heart will catch the mind out in its trick of offering momentary satisfaction which distracts that blissful moment. In that sense, a sage must dwell in inner peace in order to recognize every source of satisfaction as just another aspect of a mind game and continue to live without being swayed by its allure. In other words, every second of your life will be blissful when you learn to dwell in inner peace.

As I mentioned earlier, whether you become a philosopher or a sage depends on the extent to which you recognize the difference between the mind and the heart. Once you recognize the nobility of your heart or dwell in inner peace, you clearly see the mind for what it is—a faculty that stands apart from you. The mind is distinct from your noble heart, and the noble heart is unique to each one of us and at the same time common to us all irrespective to the image you may have cherished as a philosopher or a sage.

If you are the kind of person who tends to occasionally get carried away by the short-lived pleasure of satisfaction but recognizes that satisfaction itself is not happiness, then you are a sage. It means you have the sense of peace that dwells within you and which is attributable to your openness and your receptivity to bliss. Perhaps, up until now, you neither noticed nor recognized it as an expression of the nobility of your heart. I sincerely hope that you do so now and will be able to distinguish between momentary satisfaction and the existence of bliss – true happiness.

What I find interesting is that we will be happy when we are far from our enslaved mind and its' mental processes. Our happiness doesn't come from external rewards or praises. The external delights based on perceptions may make us satisfied for a few minutes, hours, or days, but they cannot make us happy. For Socrates, one of the great ancient philosophers—*in my assessment who bear wisdom*—happiness came from seclusion, and he said, "People confer internal success upon themselves." He further writes, "The secret of happiness, you see, is not found in seeking more, but in developing the capacity to enjoy less." The internal success he is referring to is our inner capacity to enjoy less or be happy—*inner peace.* This happiness we confer is an expression of the nobility of our heart, our receptivity to inner peace. In fact, Socrates was later recognized as a sage in the Mosaic of the Seven Sages in the National Museum of Beirut built in third century BC in Greece. This is proof that eventually a great philosopher will become a bearer of wisdom—*dwell in inner peace.*

Happiness depends upon ourselves.

—ARISTOTLE

CHAPTER 6

Happiness

YOU MAY HAVE NOW CLEARLY established that happiness and satisfaction lie at opposite ends of the continuum of pleasantness. Happiness comes from the heart and through the openness of the mind. Satisfaction is always driven by perceptions which are short lived. When questions go unanswered or cravings are not satisfied, the result will be unhappiness, frustration, or unsatisfactoriness. But when happiness pervades your inner being, it does not involve thoughts or perceptions. Happiness neither fulfills nor discounts any of your needs or cravings, but it fills you with bliss. It is independent of your cravings or needs, unconcerned with their satisfaction or the lack thereof. Therefore, happiness is not a self-centered phenomenon like satisfaction. It is universal and available for everyone to experience at will.

When happiness arises, you don't perceive any concern over satisfaction or dissatisfaction within yourself. Most likely happiness occupies your mind completely, and there is no room to think. In such a state of being, you will realize that everything arises and ceases based on your thoughts and perceptions. While it seems improbable to come across individuals who find themselves in this state and lead blissful and happy lives, it is not as rare as you may think. In each one of us there is intense happiness that we call bliss—*the nobility of our heart.* We need to elevate it.

Since you are reading this book, I am sure that you have experienced blissful moments in your life that have preserved your sanity to work on uplifting your happiness. You do have mental equilibrium to sufficiently explore your inner peace. Whether philosopher or sage, perhaps you are yet to be aware that you bear the bliss that brings lasting happiness. Often human beings fail to recognize it but appreciate and enjoy it, mistaking it for a short-lived satisfaction.

For example, you may take a vacation thinking that you are seeking satisfaction from travel, but you are truly looking for blissfulness. If you prefer amusement parks or vibrant activities for your vacation, you are looking for perceived happiness. In other words, you are pursuing satisfaction rather than happiness. If you prefer sightseeing and enjoy being with nature to admire the beauty of natural phenomenon, you are truly seeking a blissful time for peace of mind, calmness, and true happiness, not satisfaction. You are approaching your life with sage in you.

Whether humans recognize it or not, bliss is certainly a phenomenon that exists everywhere. Often lost in our thoughts, we become enslaved by our minds. We fail to recognize the bliss in our hearts, even when it surfaces from time to time. Bliss only surfaces when we are able to cut off all thoughts and pause for a moment, as we did while gazing at a tree or admiring the beauty of a sunset. These sights that move us to joy and tears are clear examples of the bliss that lies within our noble hearts and manifests itself through us. This brings us to the question of whether the noble heart itself is the bliss that exists, regardless of whether humans feel that or not. It is a question that many individuals have pondered in the past. And irrespective of whether they were philosophers or sages, their interest in the subject impelled them to investigate it with thoroughness, and in the process, they discovered universal blissfulness—*inner peace.*

You may not be aware when bliss springs through your inner essence. But it occurs more frequently than you think and goes unnoticed. You may not agree with this assessment at this stage. I encourage you to carefully examine the discussion in this chapter and recognize this with your firsthand experiences.

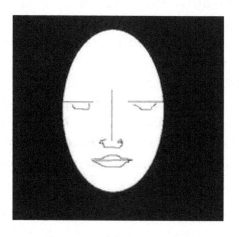

Bliss is within and beyond you...

When you examine the above image, what do you see? A face bearing a peaceful expression or an incomplete sketch? Inquiring philosophers see a sketch yet to be completed, while the sage in you infers the peace depicted in that same sketch.

While you look at this image, pause for a moment, just as you would stop and admire a colorful sunset. For an instant, you may not notice the incompleteness of the sketch because you are focused on its peaceful expression. For that fraction of a second, you are free of perceptions and respond to the picture from the bottom of your heart. That is your intuition. The peaceful expression of the drawing resembles inner peace, and a stream of bliss will flow within you as a response. However, in the very next second, your mind plays its usual tricks and obstructs your bliss with the perception that the picture is incomplete.

This image above of a face symbolizes a profound truth. The face takes its shape from the surrounding frame and the black lines within; this is like the way our thoughts formulate perceptions and contribute to our persona of self and lend definition to our character. Without the presence of the black color, we cannot recognize a face or even an image in the white space. If not disturbed by thought, emotions, and perceptions, our inner essence is like that pristine white space, blissful and peaceful. Bliss shines in us is like the color white that emanates through the black sketch of the face. Our inner essence is shared with others like the vast white surface sharing pictures, words, and sentences on this page.

The white or absence of black color on the page is a simile for bliss you experience from time to time, free from thoughts that make you happy. But mostly, it's the black lines that catch your attention, just as your thoughts, perceptions, emotions, and seeking satisfaction take precedence over your blissful essence. Because we lack the attentiveness to inner peace, we surrender to our enslaved mind. So enslaved do we become by our mental processes, we fail to appreciate the beauty and brilliance of the white surface—*inner peace*—that provides the base for our self-image. Similarly, the pursuit of satisfaction blinds you from the beauty and significance of color white—*inner peace*. Allow your inner peace to rise to the surface. That will give you the clarity of vision necessary to appreciate your inner essence. The color black represents *the mind,* and the white surface represents the happiness dormant within us – *inner peace.*

When interpreting the above image of the face, we use our own approach. Philosophers start from the image drawn with black ink and later notice the white background—*inner peace*—that gives birth to it. Sages, on the other hand, see the white background with clarity and notice the black ink forming a peaceful expression—the image of a peaceful face.

When you pause for a moment at the spectacle of a sunset or focus on a tree, a plant, or an image, you are in the process of transcending and recognizing the peace and tranquility within yourself that is undisturbed by emotional upheaval. It is imperative that we recognize this special moment in which we experience the expression of inner peace—*bliss.* If you have the courage to recognize bliss in you, you will be drawn to inner peace. Because of our inherited mental processes, we fail to give due attention to bliss and let our enslaved mind take precedence and lose our courage. Through our ignorance, we fail to recognize our latent capacity for a blissful life and forfeit an infinitely precious and attainable blissful life, the life full of happiness.

The more we are able to recognize the bliss within, the more we enhance our courage to be at peace with ourselves. Sometimes you may feel you've done enough thinking and need a break by going to a park or taking a vacation. This urge stems from your heart to remind you to be with inner peace, and I call this urge as courage or thirst for happiness. Many of us misinterpret this thirst and look for fleeting satisfaction. Underlying this urge for complete mental relaxation is the courage of our longing to be happy. I would not call this thirst as the desire for satisfaction, since it is not a conceptual seeking. But often we let our perceptions suppress our courage and bring other priorities over them mostly supported by doubt and fear.

You need to stimulate your courage to explore within by frequently recognizing the bliss springing in you. It is like filling pure and clean water by opening the faucet while emptying the dirty water from the sink. Your courage to enjoy bliss will push away all the thoughts leading to doubts and miseries. That will cleanse your mind. Bliss will fill up your mind and body like eventually the sink will be filled with pure water. You will experience true happiness.

Consider this is as another opportune moment for you to test yourself to surface the bliss within you. Spend a few seconds probing your attention deep into the inner silence, and try to relax and recognize the calm and peaceful nature within yourself. Spread that feeling to space within and around you. Ponder on this unconditional awareness and the arising calmness, joy, and happiness embracing you. This is the bliss that exists free from the interference of the enslaved mind. What you did now allows bliss to occupy within you fully. It will emanate courage in you which brings clarity of purpose of your life. With such courage you may disregard fear and consequences. It is like you go into a car-crash site to rescue injured victims without any hesitation. You defeat the tricks of the enslaved mind and go to the danger zone with a courage that is not subject to any preconceived perceptions or fear. Every situation in your life could be a site of a car- crash, yet you will face it without any hesitation, fear, and doubt. You will experience the bliss of being alive – true happiness. It is the inner peace in and around us clear from our mind.

When you have the right level of courage, you will not encounter satisfaction or dissatisfaction within yourself. You will make sure the bliss is occupying your mind completely; therefore, there will be no room for confusing thoughts. In such a state of bliss, you will realize that all miserable situations arise from conditional circumstances cannot distract your happiness. Many find themselves in this state and lead blissful lives. This is not as rare as you may think.

As mentioned, at one stage in your life, you may have experienced a courageous blissful moment. This has conserved your sanity and mental stability sufficiently to explore who you are and your inner peace. That is why you picked this book to read. Often human beings fail to recognize inner peace but benefit from it.

You may think bliss is satisfying, and it also is a fleeting phenomenon. Such thought processes are also a doing of your enslaved mind. Satisfaction and bliss are opposite sides of a coin. Satisfaction stems from the mind. Bliss stems from inner peace. When the mind dominates, we do not enjoy inner peace. When the inner peace is prominent, we distance our enslaved mind to experience the bliss of being alive. If you think bliss is satisfying, your mind is dominating to obscure the wonderful benefits of being blissful. What I am trying here is to surge your interest in inner peace to encourage and sustain your blissful sensations. Once you recognize and sustain the blissful sensations surfacing in you and realize the benefits, the courage to dwell in inner peace is inevitable.

It is like we need to go outside to see the entire house. When we are inside the house—*enslaved mind*—we cannot see its entirety. Once we see the miseries in us as the trick of our mind, we can take our attention away from it. This will open our hearts and direct you to blissful sensations. You cannot conceptualize and interpret bliss or true happiness; you need to experience it firsthand. When bliss appears, you need to pay attention and sustain it for as long as you can. If you are successful in doing so, there is no room for the enslaved mind to interfere with your true happiness.

As mentioned earlier, everything we do begins with a fleeting pause—a pause that may go unnoticed. The bliss I am referring to belongs to this pause that is undisturbed by thoughts. Bliss arises in the space between thoughts. That is the reason why thoughts or perceptions are absent when you are in the moment of bliss or being happy. Therefore, happiness is not what you get from someone or something. It is what you experience within, when your mind is clear from any thoughts or perceptions. The closer you are to recognizing bliss, the greater are your chances of being happy and at peace with yourself. As mentioned earlier, there are times when you feel you've done enough thinking and need to get away by going to a park or taking a vacation. This urge stems from your need to be left in peace or to be on your own so that you can have a quiet moment to yourself. Underlying this thirst for complete mental relaxation is the stirrings of our noble heart – *inner peace.*

In contrast, the mind always seeks to fulfill perceived happiness or satisfaction. The satisfaction—*pursuit for happiness*—is always short lived since the perception of happiness changes every moment. Your blissful experience will never end if you recognize it and allow it to flourish in you. I trust that I have probed such courage and thirst in you to follow your bliss and discover this profound true happiness.

Aristotle lived from 384 to 322 BC; he was a student of Plato in ancient Greece. Along with Plato, he is considered as a fellow philosopher. As a result, his philosophy has exerted a unique influence on almost every form of knowledge in the West. Once again in my assessment Aristotle was also a great philosopher and a bearer of wisdom rather than a seeker of wisdom, since he stated that "Happiness depends upon ourselves." This means he recognized that happiness is not something we get from outside or by conceptualizing. We need to experience happiness by ourselves, when it's springing from our noble heart. We will explore how to experience this with a philosopher in us, in the next chapter.

Explore Within

There is only one thing a philosopher can be relied upon to do, and that is to contradict other philosophers.

—William James

CHAPTER 7

Philosopher

IN THIS CHAPTER, WE WILL further explore whether the approach of a philosopher is prominent in you, and if so, how to explore inner peace with that approach. You may have already settled with the idea of a philosopher. If not, you can critically examine our discussion here and try some of the self-checks I have outlined to test and identify for yourself.

Many of us are thinkers and philosophers. A philosopher's mind is mostly dominated by conceptual theories and thinking. We question everything until a satisfactory answer is found. This is like children asking "Why?" for every answer coming from their parents. In this world, obtaining completely satisfying answers to any question is a rare occurrence indeed. As a result, many of us philosophers are driven to raise still more questions and get lost in the process. Those questions fade away only when we recognize the whole world is within us. We create our world with our thoughts and perceptions. Many of us are philosophers until we cease seeking answers externally. When we realize that seeking answers or satisfaction from outside is an endless exercise, we will explore within. This is true for all of us no matter whether we are rich or poor, male or female, and able or challenged. What matters is your ability to see within to experience the nobility of your heart.

This also reflects the views of the ancient Greeks, which I mentioned in the first chapter—a philosopher is an *eternal seeker of wisdom*: someone who always searches the truth, comes close to it, but ultimately cannot attain perfect wisdom. When philosophers try to contradict one another, they create new theories or new philosophies and never settle with others' opinions. Philosophers who continuously seek wisdom from outside always end up with contradictions. They will rarely bear the wisdom but strengthen their self-image—*ego*.

However, I find that great philosophers go beyond their self-image and become bearers of wisdom. Certain great philosophers, who were seekers of wisdom at one stage, when keeping at it with an open mind, eventually became bearers of wisdom. In my assessment René Descartes, the famous French philosopher, mathematician, and scientist who lived from 1596 to 1650, was one of them. He is known as the father of modern Western philosophy, and much of the subsequent Western philosophy is a response to his writings. Descartes refused to accept the authority of previous philosophers. You may be like him, do not want to believe in others' ideas. Descartes frequently sets his views apart from those of his predecessors. Perhaps at one stage, he changed his approach from seeking externally to exploring within. You could do the same. In my assessment, Descartes was a great philosopher who eventually dwelled in inner peace—*bearer of wisdom*. With such a transformation he recognized the difference between living with a self-image and having a blissful life with inner peace. His best-known statement "I think, therefore I am" is an expression of this transformation.

Descartes's statement implies that our thinking leads us to a self-image. If you carefully examine it, you will see he is directly addressing our self-image "I," which is made of our thoughts and perceptions—thinking. We need to apply our philosopher's approach like Descartes did. We need to recognize the obstacles and resistances that hinder blissful experience in our life. Great philosophers like Descartes have kept an open mind, challenged conceptual thinking, and explored the intuition surging from their hearts and realized that we are mind-created selves. You, on the other hand, being the slave of your mind, may be quite satisfied with what you do and enjoy seeking answers to your endless quest externally. You may never realize that you are a slave of your mind and running around like a fish swimming in the ocean, looking for the so-called ocean. We lose ourselves in a maze of questions—boost our self-image—and never accept the fact that our essence is peaceful and universal. Instead, we may persistently challenge everything that comes from the inner essence to achieve some form of perceived satisfaction from outside.

If you take pride in being a philosopher, it leads to the creation of a self-image that hinders your progress in becoming a great philosopher. Great philosophers have always kept an open mind and explored the depths of their hearts. Instead, you will challenge everything relentlessly and make your life miserable. When you see a tree or a sunset, you probably won't pause to enjoy it—experience it—but will analyze it in your perennial quest for answers. Follow some simple exercises here and in the upcoming chapters and examine whether you feel differently next time when you encounter similar situations.

> Even a simple matter like a child playing in the dirt may be the subject of your judgment and rejection at present. You may take the opportunity to express your aversion—shout at the child—and thereby build up a satisfying self-image by thinking you are helping the child. You may think you are a caring person by wishing better hygiene for the child. You reject the child's happiness. That is the minute-level judgment that I refer to as a philosophical argument - *friction*. On the other hand, you may be glad that the child is having fun with dirt and have no friction at all with the incident. In that case, you are more of a sage than a philosopher since you shared the child's joy. You had no problem with the child's action, and you inferred within, and hopefully experienced the same joy or blissful sensation as the child.

You may assume that many things happening in the world are wrong, and you alone have the solutions that will make this world a perfect place to live. It may not occur to you that while your solution may temporarily satisfy your perception, the reality may be quite different for the rest of the world. This is because your mind deceives you into the perception that only your solution will work. So, you carry on the quest for the satisfaction that has no end, unable to distinguish between conceptual thinking and wondrous experience, the mind and the heart. With your approach as a philosopher you try to conceptualize everything. With this approach you will not find the answers unless you keep an open mind for all possibilities. Like Descartes did do not fixated with one view, be open to all possibilities including what you are experiencing right now in reading this book.

Spend some time to discover the peace within you. Open your mind to all possibilities, including the fact that it is not always the world that needs to change. It could well be that you yourself need to change too. Devote more time to changing yourself rather than putting efforts to change others. This change not necessarily needs to be large scale. It can be simple and minute as paying attention to space between two thoughts. Then gradually the path to your inner peace will open up before you. Great philosophers discovered this truth in a unique way and sought to correct the flaws. They saw the reality within themselves instead of attempting to correct what they perceived as flaws in others.

Once again, if you are a philosopher, you question the external implications of most situations you encounter, searching for the best comprehensible answer. This approach seeks that the answer is equally compatible with the stirrings of your mind. This is your confused mind that needs to reason any situation. This approach often ends up with more questions and more quests that could not be answered during one lifetime. Many of us are in that state and lost in the mind game and seek answers from external sources and end up with frustrations. Instead, we could get answers by exploring within. We need to infer how any situation relates and impacts us and resolve solutions within. This is experiencing what is happening rather than having years of debates about it. In other words, knowing by experience rather than satisfying with conceptualized beliefs. You can experience it right now. No need to spend a life time to get this wondaful sensation – true happiness.

My attempt here is to penetrate the sage in you so you can open your heart to distance from your mind game to see the philosopher in you. We will continue to explore within, probing very deeply without prejudice so that we can recognize our common bond. We will recognize the self-image—*enslaved mind*—for its worth, and thereby we will be able to distance from it to dwell in inner peace. Once you make these practices a habit, you will be able to recognize inner peace in you, in the midst of any circumstances.

From ancient times, individuals have followed a path that has led them to *recognize* the true nature of the heart and dwell in inner peace. Consequently, they lived a peaceful and blissful life. I used the word "recognize" here because our attention is the one that should dwell in inner peace. It is not an "understanding" that is always relative to what we think and -conceptualize—the process shapes our enslaved minds. "Understanding" is a making of the mind. When you recognize with wise attention, you experience it firsthand. If you are a philosopher, you need to shift your attention from conceptual thinking to experiential reality.

When you were a child, you did not believe any of the things that your parents tried to convince you. You were curious and wanted to experience everything. As a toddler you picked up things and tasted them to experience what they were, even dirt on the floor. You were never convinced that fire will burn and hurt you until you put your finger into the flame of a candle. But when we grow older, we start believing in others' opinions. So much so, we get emotionally attached to them and make our life miserable. We get deeply attached to them and are never happy anymore like we were in our childhood.

Pause your reading and contemplate on your childhood. Remember how much freedom you enjoyed during those days. You had no worries, commitments, or goals to achieve. You ran around, explored, and experimented with an open mind to understand everything in and around you. You learned a lot that cannot be forgotten. You enjoyed your life to your fullest while learning yourself and your surroundings, until your elders planted an idea that you need to become someone. Someone who is respected by your society. This opinion of others makes you think fearfully to achieve such a mind-made goal, which gradually and surely takes away your happiness.

This is happening to children earlier than before in this information age with many ambitions induced by their parents. Contemplate on the joyfulness you enjoyed in your childhood and trace forward and see when you lost that blissfulness. It may have happened gradually, but for sure, it started with someone else's opinion. Your thoughts and perceptions wrapped around that opinion. Since then you are identifying yourself with that and perusing fleeting satisfaction – *conceptual happiness*. You may be satisfied with something for a short time but look for greater satisfaction since your perceptions are renewing. You can never be happy like a child but may satisfy for a short time.

As mentioned earlier, irrespective of the petty differences that we conceptually cling to, we humans are one kind with equal capabilities while our style of approach to life may differ. Many of us are thinkers, hence philosophers, while there is also a sage in us to a certain extent. Seeking satisfaction dominates in many philosophers' mind. In this world, obtaining completely satisfying answers to any question is a rare occurrence indeed. As a result, many of us philosophers are driven to raise still more questions and get lost in the process. Once we were children full of joy and happiness. When we get older, this joy and happiness evaded from us and replaced by our intellect that we gather from books and other's opinions.

William James was a leading thinker of the late nineteenth century, one of the most influential philosophers, and has been known as the "Father of American psychology." He was the first educator to offer a psychology course in the United States as a psychologist and a philosopher. His famous quote "There is only one thing a philosopher can be relied upon to do, and that is to contradict other philosophers" sums up the approach of a philosopher. As we discussed, you will not find lasting happiness but fleeting satisfaction if you take this approach. Unless you have an open mind, it is difficult to see an end of this quest. Instead, you can sensibly analyze life situations and respond to them with your heartfelt intuition. If you do so, you will recognize the noble nature of your heart and live a happy life. In my view, the sages do have this inclination from their birth. The philosophers need to find their way to get such inclination with some effort.

Explore Within

The primary cause of unhappiness is never the situation but your thoughts about it.

—ECKHART TOLLE

Explore Within

CHAPTER 8

Sage

YOU MAY HAVE ALREADY RECOGNIZED the sage in you by responding with compassion to the child who plays in the dirt—the incident we discussed in the last chapter. You saw the child in you, did not react, instead inferred and responded that the child is having fun in the dirt. If philosophical arguments and conceptual theories are not for you, and you know there is a reason for everything, then you are in the category of sage while you may have a philosopher in you to a lesser degree.

The Buddha was one of the great sages who lived around 500 BC. Even in this modern day, his insight influences many people in recognizing life's purpose to live peacefully. Many scholars categorize the Buddha as a philosopher and his teachings as a philosophy rather than a path, religion, or a way of life. When you examine his biography, he had every external indulgence as a prince, and initially he was forced to seek answers in the outside world. In his youth he encountered inner peace and realized that seeking within is the only path to liberate oneself from the enslaved mind. The Buddha began his teaching, *a path to overcome the enslaved mind*, based on the firsthand experience he gained through his practice—after awakening—rather than based on conceptualized philosophy. His teaching is to recognize and be aware that the "Mind is the forerunner of life" and awaken to a blissful life, free from the sufferings created by our mind.

A similar message is delivered in different forms by most teachings of common religions as well—that is, be with god, be in the present, liberation or salvation. Therefore, you do not have to change your faith or path that you have already chosen to follow your own heart and dwell in inner peace.

In my assessment, Eckhart Tolle, born in 1948—the author of the best-selling book *Power of Now*—is one of the greatest sages in this modern era. He teaches to be in the present, free from the mind-made self, with its heaviness, its problems, which live in the unsatisfying past and the fearful future. He was a seeker who pursued his search by studying philosophy, psychology, and literature, and he graduated from the University of London. He was a postgraduate researcher at Cambridge University; then he stopped pursuing his doctorate after his sudden inner transformation at the age of twenty-nine. He began to feel a strong underlying sense of peace in any situation. He teaches with firsthand experience of inner peace. Tolle writes that "the most significant thing that can happen to a human being is the separation process of thinking and awareness" and that awareness is "the space in which thoughts exist." This space is inner peace, rather the nobility of your heart.

A sage is in virtue a clam and composed person. You may have noticed a few of those type in your society, or you could be one of them. If you see things quite differently from others and always see that there is a reason for any situation and it is to be accepted as it is, you are far from a philosopher.

If you tend to get carried away with the short-lived pleasures but occasionally recognize such satisfaction itself does not have much worth, then you are a sage who dislikes the enslaved mind to a certain degree. In your heart you know that something in you is pulling you into a territory you do not wish for. It is your longing for satisfaction pulling you off from your happiness. Therefore, even if you have the qualities of a sage, the enslaved mind will continue to picture a fleeting satisfaction is better and bring unhappiness to your life. You may be satisfied for a brief time, and once it has ended, you will suffer and seek further satisfaction. You may gather and accumulate vivid perceptions and memories of things and conditions around you and cling to them inadvertently and fall into the mind's trap. Blinded by those traps, you discriminate everything and seek fleeting satisfaction. By clinging to specific views, perceptions, and expectations, you are strengthening your self-image to reject others and your own happiness.

Examine within; if you see there is a reason behind for any situation, short-lived pleasure is not for you, and you prefer peace in you and nature, you are far from a common philosopher. If your self-image is an onion, the approach you may take would not be to peel it off by pulling off each skin of the onion, but to cut it in half and investigate all layers from inside out. Spend a few moments and examine who you are and what approach you prefer as it comes from your inner essence. Do not let your enslaved mind suppress your intuition; draw your attention to inner peace and identify your inner peace over short-lived pleasure. It is the pleasantness you feel free of agitation and tension in the body. This smooth sensation will surge in you and spread all over you and to the surrounding. You are experiencing true happiness.

You may presume that you are a sage, capable of looking into the depths of the heart often to recognize the peace within. You may be fascinated with the silence of the dawn and enjoy the calmness while enjoying the chirping of birds as the only disturbance to inner peace. You may be a person who meditates a few times and sees yourself as a saint. You may be a priest who imagines yourself a sage or closer to becoming a one. You may pause before a tree or gaze at the sunset and relax for a while, feeling satisfied, and think you touched inner peace. However, as long as the concept of satisfaction takes precedence in your mind, your self-image remains, and neither meditation nor priesthood is going to transform you into a great sage.

When the inner peace is sustained at a higher degree, we refer to that as bliss. The sense of peace that dwells within you is attributable to your openness and your receptivity to bliss. You cannot conceptualize and interpret bliss; you need to experience it firsthand. When bliss appears, you need to pay attention and sustain it for as long as you can. If you are successful in doing so, there is no room for the enslaved mind to interfere with your true happiness.

If possible, go outside in the dawn and spread your attention to the silence and embrace the freshness and calmness in the surroundings. You could do this while in the bed just after you wake up as well. You can recognize the ease and pleasant condition and inner peace in you by embracing the surrounding freshness and calmness in the bedroom. Dwell in it and pay attention to occasional disturbances like a bird's chirp or a clock ticking. When your base is silence and stillness—*inner peace*—your emotions, perceptions, and thoughts are like the birds' chirps in the silent dawn. You will clearly recognize that those thoughts are not part of you, like you have recognized a bird's calls or a clock ticking is a distance occurring. Our thoughts and perceptions are like the surrounding noises. When we pay attention to them, they become our own thoughts. When you dwell in inner peace, you can clearly distance the noise— *thoughts*—from the calm and quiet surroundings. You can let go of them as you did with the birds' calls or the clock ticking by paying attention to inner peace. Try this exercise for a few minutes and see how deep you can take your attention. The bliss in you will surge within and flourish all over your body. You will experience happiness in the true sense.

In contrast, the mind always seeks to fulfill perceived happiness or satisfaction. Philosophers are constantly in this rat race. If you are a sage, occasionally your mind may carry you away with a myriad of thoughts and interrupt your happiness. If you are a true sage, you will recognize this and bring back your attention to inner peace. This inner peace is the noble nature of our heart. Perhaps, up until now, you neither noticed nor recognized it as an expression of the nobility of your heart. If you recognize it and allow it to flourish in you, your blissful experience will last long. If you recognize bliss more frequently in your life, you should consider yourself as a sage.

The human mind is such a powerful faculty—created with thoughts and perceptions—and is the forerunner of life. It can distract even certain sages' inner peace and calmness. It can turn a person into a monster and make that person suffer from delusions. If you think of yourself as a sage simply because you have cherished that image in your mind and cling to that image, you are more of a thinker than an individual who bears wisdom and dwells in inner peace. It may not be apparent and could not be recognized until you try a few of self-tests to explore within.

Therefore, regardless of who you are, you need to learn how to differentiate the mind and the heart and recognize how to dwell in inner peace. The closer you recognize the nobility of your heart, the greater the possibility that you will become a great philosopher or sage.

> When you are free from your thoughts, you will be calm as undisturbed water. Focus on a mirror like a lake that has clear and clam surface of the water. You must clear all mind-created distractions—thoughts, perceptions, memories, and emotions. This will open your heart to see the world as it is, just as you would see the un-distorted reflection of the surroundings and sky on the still waters. It is as you would notice birds' chirp through the silence of the dawn. You will dwell in inner peace.

The clarity and the stillness of the water emphasize the sharpness and accuracy of nature's mirror image, which renders objects and their reflections distinguishable. Similarly, when your inner peace and stillness prevail in your heart, bliss will flourish. You will be able to experience the reality of the world as it is, undistorted by your mind's distractions. As a sage or a philosopher, your goal would be to achieve clarity of your heart and allow the peace within to reign and usher blissful living.

The extent to which you recognize the nobility of the heart depends on how far you have travelled in your quest to become a philosopher or sage. Although you may be unaware of it, recognizing the bliss that dwells within your noble heart brings you the well-being. This is the underlined reward that you have been seeking for all along. You are to free from your mind no matter whether you are a philosopher or a sage.

With your sage's approach, you need to examine whether you are genuinely identifying the sage in you or if you are pretending. Your mind may project a persona of a sage while you are suffering internally.

Examine the deepest level with integrity to see whether you are cheating yourself with the influence of your enslaved mind. Do you occasionally get angry or frustrate? Then you are a slave of your mind. Similarly, your intention may be to do good in the world by becoming an activist. Consider what it does to you. You are building friction on others' ideas and trying to change others rather than changing your attitude, which creates an aversion in you. Irrespective of the outcome of your action, you suffered from friction and short-lived pleasure. However, eventually what you did was fatten your layer of aversion with others.

Similarly, some people believe in spending money and time doing good deeds in the expectation of merits, satisfactions, recognitions, or from fear of consequences after death. If this is the case, you are ultimately looking for satisfaction. As long as you are expecting something in return, doing such good deeds are tricks of your mind and you are looking for self-satisfaction. You cannot get true happiness by doing things expecting something in return. It should come from your heart with a companion to feel true happiness.

If you recognize that you are more of a sage, you need to be honest and respond to your intuition without doubt and fear. Integrity is the key to being open to your heart and recognizing all the layers of self-image so that you can be like a lake with clear and calm water. You will respond to any distress that comes to you like a mirror image of the surrounding nature reflecting on still water. There won't be any impact on your inner peace, and it will not be distressing, but a welcome reminder of the enslaved mind. We discussed this in detail in the chapter titled "Satisfaction."

Here is another test for you. As a sage you may be quick to read someone's facial expression. When you see someone making a face for something you did or said, you may instantly run through your thought process, leading you to judge and react. It may lead to arguments and quarrels. This is again friction, a flaw in you. Making a face may have happened intentionally or unintentionally. That person may be regretting their own unintentional reaction. Still you react to it, and you may verbalize it and get into a quarrel with that person. The friction or aversion is a flaw in you and not in others. So, be attentive to all your reactions and identify them as your flaws and correct them then and there. You will recognize the ease and sense of bliss coming through you when the friction is absent. Once you master this, you will be able to take your attention away from the pain from a blood-drawing needle prick and smile at the nurse. Or else you will be able to compassionately look and smile at a mosquito that is drawing your blood to satisfy its hunger.

Before you turn the page, I would like to emphasize the fundamental aspect of our expedition. As I mentioned earlier, philosophical and logical arguments are based on our fleeting thoughts and perceptions. They may satisfy us briefly but will never make us happy. However, our firsthand experiences will never fade away from us. When we experience inner peace, we recognize the nobility of our heart to cherish our well-being. I trust the self-checks in this book help you to recognize your unique approach to your life. With that base we will further explore our inner peace in the next chapter.

Further, when Eckhart Tolle stated that "the primary cause of unhappiness is never the situation but your thoughts about it" in his book *A New Earth: Awakening to Your Life's Purpose*, he clearly pinpointed the root cause for our unhappiness. When we mull on confusing thoughts we suffer. When you start thinking you may not notice this, but when it snowballs to a myriad of confusing thoughts, it becomes a misery. Therefore, when you are looking for happiness, do not think about it; instead, turn to your noble heart, which is full of joy and happiness.

There is no path to happiness:
Happiness is the path.

—THE BUDDHA

Explore Within

CHAPTER 9

Inner Peace

I TRUST THAT YOU now know to what extent you have the philosopher and sage in you. While reading this you may have shifted your approach between either extreme. Or you may feel you are at a certain point in between them. These extremes are like the edges of the balancing bar of a traditional balanced scale. If you lean towards either edge, it will tilt to that side. Likewise, if you cherish either of the approaches, eventually you will become a great philosopher or a sage. From the edge of that extreme you will fall into the reservoir of inner peace. We need to have the courage to walk all the way to any edge of our approach to find our happiness and dwell in inner peace. Therefore, I would like to extend our expedition a little further to explore the way to recognize our noble heart to dwell in inner peace to enjoy true happiness.

True happiness is living a life without stress, problems, doubt, and fear. This can be achieved by dwelling in inner peace. We need to learn how to eliminate the friction inside of us and allow the bliss to surge through our noble heart. When you are experiencing bliss and sustaining it, you are peaceful. If you sustain this peacefulness – *inner peace* – you will respond to a situation instead of reacting to it. Our happiness depends on the extent to which we recognize and follow the bliss inside of us. This will empower you to experience true happiness – *inner peace* – and respond to every situation rather than reacting to it.

If you are pursuing happiness, you are chasing happiness without experiencing it. Instead we need to detect peace within us and usher our own happiness in every moment. The fundamental obstacle to this is a sense of satisfaction that is created by our enslaved mind. When we usher our bliss, this obstacle will fade away and the nobility of our heart will open up for us. Once you make this a habit, you will be responding to situations rather than reacting to them. Hence there will be no stress, problems, doubt, and fear in your life. With such an approach, you will be able to return to the state of blissfulness you were born with to experience the bliss of being alive. My attempt here is to help you get to that state of living.

You must surely have noticed by now that we have been talking about the mind and the heart as two separate faculties inside of us. One could even say they are not faculties but representatives of two types of approaches—*a philosopher and a sage*. The common definition of a philosopher describes an individual who challenges all ideas and chases satisfaction, or one who seeks a fleeting sense of happiness. Philosophers mostly dwell in their minds and, occasionally, recognize their hearts. Sages, on the contrary, live in their hearts, with little room in their minds for satisfaction or disappointment. They accept the prevailing conditions around them and try to adapt themselves accordingly. Yet, their minds have the potential to cheat them of that ideal state of being with nobility by creating perceptions and streams of thought that can rob them of their inner peace.

To provide a different perspective, I would like you to explore memories from your past and see whether you can endorse your discovery of who you are. In the course of your journey through life, it is quite probable that you have asked yourself the following questions: Who am I? Why was I born? What am I doing on this planet? My experience tells me that there are two kinds of thought processes behind those questions.

Have you ever pondered the fact that the universe has a common structure or pattern? In fact, the day you grasped the principle underlying the system of planets revolving around the sun, perhaps your instinct told you that this principle is applicable to everything around you. Think of the discovery that every atom operates on similar principles, with electrons moving around the nucleus. Now, consider that every single cell around you also operates in accordance with the same principles. Would that increase your fascination with the idea that was dormant within you all along from your birth? If you follow your instinct, you will discover that everything around you follows the same fundamental principle. You could, in fact, be reading this book to discover the answers to the curiosity that beset you. Sounds familiar? It's the seed of a sage that you inherited despite approaching life as a philosopher.

If that is not the case with you, your experiences may have taught you that there is more to this world than what meets the eye. Your faith or other compulsions may have led you to believe that there is a divine force behind everything that happens in this world. You may have been seeking satisfaction from the outside world like a philosopher. Nevertheless, your inner experience was probably real enough to convince you that there is a universal principle governing everything around you. You would like to be in harmony with nature and experience the comfort in life you achieve with that attitude—an attitude guided by the noble nature of your heart. This is the quality of a sage surging in you, although you think you are more of a philosopher.

In both cases if you continue your quest, you will come to the same realization: whether it is based on instinct or faith, you recognize that there is a common principle governing the whole world. This is in every human being, from birth, which gradually leads them to recognize their noble heart. Therefore, whether you are a philosopher or a sage, your noble heart shares a common ground on this universal principle. If we go back to the analogy of the sketch of a face once more, its white surface represents the universal principle of inner peace. When interpreting the drawing on it, in black ink, we build our self-image. Philosophers start from the image drawn with black ink and later notice the white background that gives birth to it. Sages, on the other hand, see the white background with clarity, and then notice the black ink forming an image on the surface.

As we mentioned earlier, satisfaction is based on self-image. It surfaces in your mind through the creation of images, just as black ink forms an image on white paper. Inner peace is an image-free phenomenon that arises in your heart, like white paper without marks or images. The answer to the question, "Who are you?" depends on the predominance of your cloud of perceptions. In other words, your self-image and how much of that black ink is covering the white surface is *inner peace.*

However, the great philosophers of this world, unhindered by limitations and unbiased by perceptions, recognize the nature of the heart buried deep within. In order to achieve greatness and enjoy a blissful life, a philosopher needs to explore matters inward and examine every aspect of the questions surfacing in their mind. This dissolves the self-image that was created by the mind to reveal the noble heart that you were born with as a human being.

If you are a sage, you should recognize the noble nature of your heart frequently. You may be experiencing bliss and inner peace intermittently. But if you are a great sage, you will never become a slave to your mind because you would recognize the nobility of your heart every second of your life and be at peace with yourself forever—*dwelling in inner peace.*

As a philosopher or a sage, you will, from time to time, be able to touch your heart's inherent nobility and experience the peace within. As long as you never cease to do so and continue your journey toward the ultimate happiness, you will keep yourself open to the possibility of becoming a great philosopher or a great sage. As you make progress in your quest, the degree of receptivity to inner peace will increase in you.

Your enthusiasm for blissful living is the courage you need to enhance; some of the techniques provided in this book are to surface this courage. Practicing these techniques will assist you to dive deeper into inner peace. Once you see the results, you will get encouraged to continue practicing. Then you will be able to instantly *respond* to a situation rather than *react* to it. We have already examined within and practiced a few exercises to improve our skills to recognize the bliss inside us. With that skill we can reach inner peace in any situation like a stone rapidly sinking into the bottom of the lake. It is like going through a portal to dwell in inner peace. When you totally recognize inner peace, the rest of the activities and situations are just vibrations in the outer ring. You are still, peaceful, and free of doubt and fear.

A person who spontaneously jumps into a raging stream of water to rescue a stranger is interrupting the myriad of thoughts in their head; overcoming fear and doubt instantly with such intuitive courage coming from the noble heart. You have developed that level of courage. I trust that you can now dwell in inner peace directly by repeatedly recognizing your confusing thoughts in every situation.

You may still not be convinced with the experience you got, just by trying the exercises we did so far. This may be your logical mind obstructing your happiness. Here, I am sharing another practice I use to follow bliss and distance myself from the enslaved mind and be free from miseries.

Start your day by paying attention and embracing the calmness in the dawn. During the rest of the day recall that peaceful and blissful moment frequently. With that base, you will see where your attention is; is it creating frictions, seeking satisfaction or content with bliss? After a few days it will become second nature to you. You will see the consequences or drawbacks of confusing thoughts that cling to perceptions and create friction with others or in difficult situations. Once you experience it firsthand you will be convinced that such thoughts interrupt your happiness. This will be engrained in your heart and will pop up frequently like a song stuck in your head. Once you experience such convincing proof of happiness, peaceful living is inevitable! You are experiencing the bliss of being alive.

True happiness is experiencing the bliss of being alive. This is enabled by *responding* to every situation rather than *reacting*. As mentioned earlier, it is simple to say, but hard to execute. The techniques I have outlined in this book are to cultivate the skills that will help you to recognize your inner peace. This will empower you to respond to any situation and be happy in all circumstances. When you learn how to respond with bliss to every fraction of a second in any situation, true happiness is inevitable. This true happiness is permanent and persists even during the chaos. When you are true with inner peace, every incident is another occurrence in this present moment which does not happen in the past or will happen in the future. So, you should live with it happily. You have no choice, yet the mind may think otherwise.

If you are pursuing fleeting happiness, you will never arrive because you are looking for it intellectually rather than being with it. True happiness is not conventional pleasure or satisfaction based on perceptions. True happiness is a sense of bliss that comes from your inner peace. When your attention is free from distractions, you will experience this clearly. In other words, happiness occurs when you are free from all distractions, especially when you evade friction and the clinging coming from your enslaved mind. Our true happiness is free from inner agitation and irritations that bother us irrespective of the circumstances of our life. Things we accumulated throughout our life, either as material things or metaphysical longings, cannot make us happy.

With your sage approach you may try a more dedicated practice to explore your inner peace. Next time you are relaxing on the beach or on your recliner chair, try this exercise. If you do this right, I assure you that you will frequently repeat this until you dwell in inner peace.

When you are in the reclining position, relax your body as much as you can. Take a deep breath, and when exhaling without any effort, relax your entire body. Your attention should travel from forehead to toe with a relaxing sensation. Do this for a couple more times. Next let the breathing happen without any effort; that is, do not take a deep breath. Just breathe in as usual, without any tension or effort, but pay attention to it and follow the air bubble coming in with a soothing sensation through your nostrils and into the lungs. With this you will be relaxing your mind. With your exhale, relax your body as you did during the first few breaths. Let this effortless breathing and relaxing calm your mind and body for a while until you feel lighter and freer from thoughts. By this time your eyes should be half or fully closed. Eventually with such relaxation, your attention will settle in the light of pleasantness over your head – like a halo. You will feel that you are free from agitation and tightness in your mind and body. Inquisitively pay attention to that silence and pleasantness in you and follow it as it spreads through your head to the surrounding space. You will experience inner peace at its best. As mentioned earlier, if you do this correctly, you will be naturally encouraged to repeat this until you constantly dwell in inner peace.

The Buddha, who dissects the mind in his teachings, takes happiness and puts the greatest emphasis on people finding fulfillment in the experience of living rather than arriving. When he said, "There is no path to happiness: Happiness is the path," there is no goal for the Buddha; you make your happiness at present by awakening now, not at the end of your journey of life. The Buddha taught how to purify the mind by distance yourself from mind-created sufferings so that you will be happy.

His teaching is to be happy in the present by recognizing the cause of suffering—the mind. In other words, become a bearer of wisdom rather than one seeking it. So, irrespective of your approach—*either a philosopher or a sage*—you will find the nobility of your heart—*in inner peace*—to experience the bliss of being alive!

When you identify yourself as a philosopher or a sage, you can easily liberate from it. You should not be fixated to any self-image that will limit your true happiness. I mean you must release that image to embrace inner peace. When you dwell in inner peace free of any conceptual thinking, then you are universal.

In fact, all religions give the same message. In Michael A. Singer's book *The Untethered Soul: The Journey Beyond Yourself*, he states:

"In the mystical Gospel of John, Christ says, "That they all may be ones; as thou, Father, art in me, and I in thee, that they also may be made perfect in one..." (John 17:21-23). So it was thought in the Hindu Vedas: so it was taught in the Jewish Kabbalah; so it was written by the great Sufi mystic poets; and so it was taught in all the great religious traditions of all time."

This "oneness" is your noble heart which you share in the form of inner peace. Here, there is no differentiation such as you and me. Both you and I are the same as the oxygen in the air! Bring your awareness – *wise attention* – to that level, and you will be dwelling in the reservoir of inner peace.

The secret to finding the deeper level in the other is finding the deeper level in yourself, without finding it in yourself, you cannot see it in the other.

—ECKHART TOLLE

Explore Within

CHAPTER 10

Vow

I HOPE THIS EXPERIENTIAL JOURNEY helps you to discover who you are and the path to inner peace. You must have noticed that our primary objective was to explore the depths of your heart and the peace that resides within. In other words, this exploration allows you to recognize life as it is and get closer to your inner peace. The greater the peace in you, the better you can recognize the bliss within your heart and in others. The closer you can get to your noble heart, the more you will live your life blissfully, enjoying health, and peace of mind in this challenging world.

When you pause and focus on something free of perceptions, you will see it in its entirety. Your instinct is at work, and your heart is involved. It is a state of being that is blissful. Your mind does not take precedence in this experience; you are not a slave of your mind during this period, although this could be a fraction of a second. When you regularly touch this blissfulness, eventually, your attention dwells in inner peace. It will be like a song stuck in your head. The peace inside of you will pop up constantly. With such unwavering inner peace, you will be able to accept situations as they are, wisely adapting yourself to them, and using them for the betterment of yourself and others. You will interact with every person in your life with harmony. This is a soft skill that you can use at work, at home, and any other challenging situations. You will respond to them with wisdom. You will not react to other's omissions and commissions. You will become a bearer of wisdom.

It is the way of all great philosophers and sages. Think of those whose names are familiar to you and try to discover how they succeeded in maintaining a deep level of serenity throughout their lives. The answer lies in their ability to respond to all situations and conditions, even if the situation seems unfavorable at the time. As a result, they led contented lives, replete with health, and bliss that reflected the peace within.

I trust that you are already determined to become a better philosopher or sage to dwell in inner peace. When your mind is as calm as undisturbed water, your cognitive ability is at its most intense. Consequently, you can see the world as it is with an open heart, just as you would see the undistorted reflection of trees, hills, and the sky on still waters or as you would notice birds chirp through the silence of the dawn. Similarly, when inner peace and stillness prevail in your heart, bliss will flourish. You will be able to see the world at a distance, undistorted by your mind's tricks. As a sage or a philosopher, your will should be to achieve clarity of mind. This will allow the peace within to surge through your heart. This willpower is the courage that I referred to earlier as the key to opening your heart. Although you may be unaware of it, the energy field that governs this whole universe is the inner peace within you. Recognize the inner peace that dwells within you. This inner peace makes you a great person, and that is the reward that you're seeking as a human being.

From ancient times to this day, many philosophers and sages have dwelled in inner peace and shared it in many ways. Most of the prevailing religions are fundamentally based on the same pathway. I find that there is a common ground in these pathways that resemble the *ancient path* that is referred to in many religions with different words. The modern-day spiritual teachings emphasize something similar to mindfulness or attention to the present moment. You may have learned that "the present moment" is the only moment that we have, that the past is history, and that future events are fantasy. This again is another way to encourage you to experience the bliss of being alive—*inner peace*. If you deeply investigate this, you will recognize that this is embedded in all prevailing, peace-loving religious and spiritual teachings. Therefore, you do not have to change your faith to dwell in inner peace and to be happy.

Having read this far, I hope you now recognize your inner peace and see your heart as an independent faculty, distinct from your mind. I would like to urge you to practice the exercises we did throughout this expedition to reaffirm who you are. Explore your inner peace and learn to recognize your heart's inherent nobility. That profound experience will serve as the key to becoming a great sage or philosopher. With your reading and experience of looking at a tree, a plant, or a sunset with complete attention or listening to a bird's song in the thick silence of the dawn, you will experience mental clarity. This will give rise to your inner peace and allow you to comprehend the mirror image of reality in this world. That is the nobility of your heart that will guide you to peace and happiness.

If you are taking the philosopher's approach, first you need to eliminate identity with your self-image. This includes all discriminatory identities such as nationality, race, and gender. This will give you the freedom to respond without friction. You will be able to interact with other people without prejudice. You will have a clear mind to listen to any ideas with an open heart. This empowers you to respond calmly to any situation. You will respond to all situations like nature's reflection in calm water. You will not react with preconceived ideas. In fact, reaction stems from our deep-rooted perceptions. We react to frightening sounds with our survival instincts. This is built into our DNA – through our evolutionary process – as a defense mechanism. Our enslaved mind elevates this to reject and react and defend all mind made identities and perceptions. That is taking our survival techniques too far. In the extreme this can lead to mass scale fighting and killing. At the micro level you do this in your enslaved mind based on your perceptions. You can eliminate reactions to such mind made emotions by reducing the friction and clinging in you. Then you can match the experiences by which great philosophers have lived. You have already discovered whether you can do so and how far you are along that path. Once you eliminate friction and clinging you will enjoy inner peace. Then you too will respond to any situation like a great philosopher without making it a problem or a stressful event.

This book shows you how to work on your own and progress along the path that will lead you to recognize your noble heart – *inner peace*. When you experience that reality firsthand, it will fill your mind with bliss and happiness. That is the inner peace we all share, just like we share oxygen in the air.

You are reading this book to find out who you are because you wanted to either satisfy yourself or bring peace to your mind by discovering your true self. Was it just satisfaction or a fleeting moment of bliss? Whatever the case, I urge you to go deeper and discover to what extent you can recognize your inner peace. That is what you were truly looking for as you read this book. The purpose of every word in this book is to reward you with inner peace.

This empowers you to respond to any situation and be happy in all circumstances. You will recognize all situations are like nature's reflection in calm water or a bird's chirp in the stillness of dawn. Your vow should be to ensure that each event in your life makes an impression on your heart, just as it would calm your mind. As mentioned earlier, true happiness is experiencing the bliss of being alive. This is enabled by *responding* to every situation rather than *reacting* to it. What you need is unwavering inner peace. Once you have succeeded in doing so, you can match the experiences by which great philosophers and sages have lived. You have already discovered whether you can do so and how far you are along that path. Explore further the noble heart within you, and dive deep into the depths of inner peace. For this is something you alone need to do for yourself. No one else can do it on your behalf. Do not be a slave to external stimuli and others' opinions; distance yourself from your enslaved mind, and enjoy inner peace if you haven't already experienced it.

The longer you hold on to the awareness of your heart's nobility, the greater the possibility that your inner peace will grow. Therefore, keep your attention focused on your inner peace, and make it last as long as you can which serve you better. As I have learned through firsthand experience, when your experience of the heart deepens, your mind will open up and you will become more receptive to the bliss within. With such openness, clarity, and bliss permeating your mind, the decisions you make in life will be in perfect harmony with your social and economic environment. The mere fact that bliss pervades your mind will ensure that you prosper beyond your imagination in terms of health, and well-being.

As Eckhart Tolle aptly said, "The secret to finding the deeper level in the other is finding the deeper level in yourself, without finding it in yourself, you cannot see it in the other."

The deeper level you see in others is the inner peace that you share with them. When you see the universal nature of your noble heart, your compassion, empathy, and love for yourself and others will become inevitable.

The peace within you will be evident to others as they recognize the change that has come over you. It will lead others to seek the same levels of peace, health, and well-being that are enriching your life. Just as planets revolve around the sun, your inner peace will attract peace-loving hearts around you. They too will recognize their inner peace and serve as the nucleus for other peace-loving souls. And so, from one to the other, inner peace will radiate to create many peaceful souls in this world. With that, we can evolve into a civilization that reveres peace and wisdom, a peace-loving world. As a philosopher or a sage, I trust you will vow to ensure this happens!

Explore Within

RECOMMENDED READINGS

Hanh, Thich Nhat. *Peace Is Every Step: The Path of Mindfulness in Everyday Life.* New York: Bantam Books, 1991.

Harris, Dan. *10% Happier: How I Tamed the Voice in My Head, Reduced Stress Without Losing My Edge, and Found Self-Help That Actually Works—A True Story.* Ann Arbor, MI: Farmington Hills, 2014.

Karmapa XVII. *The Heart Is Noble: Changing the World from the Inside Out.* Boston, MA: Shambhala, 2013.

Sadhguru. *Inner Engineering: A Yogi's Guide to Joy.* New York: Penguin Random House LLC, 2016.

Singer, Michael A. *The Untethered Soul: The Journey Beyond Yourself.* New Hampshire Publication Inc. Oakland, CA, 2007

Tolle, Eckhart. *A New Earth: Awakening to Your Life's Purpose.* New York: PLUME, a member of Penguin Group USA Inc., 2006.

Tolle, Eckhart. *Power of Now: A Guide to Spiritual Enlightenment.* Vancouver, Canada: Namaste Publishing Inc., 1997.

ABOUT THE AUTHOR

N. T. Hettigei's (Nandasena T. Hettigei) life journey started in a rural village in Sri Lanka. As he has navigated through personal and professional challenges in Sri Lanka, New Zealand, and the United States, he attributes his success to inner peace. He is a retired certified public accountant and an IT audit and security professional, who gave up on his career to pursue his aspiration of sharing his experience of inner peace.

He confesses that it is the inner peace that has helped him enjoy doing the right thing during his whole life, including his forty-year professional career, and he sincerely wishes that this book will help others to find their inner peace to resolve the challenges in their life.

Made in the USA
Monee, IL
06 November 2019

16387462R00075